PREHISTORY AND THE DINOSAURS

PREHISTORY
AND THE DINOSAURS

Robert Muir Wood

Horus Editions

Designed by Paul Richards
Cover design by Richard Rowan
Illustrated by Tim Hayward, Janos Marffy, Shane Marsh,
Mike Saunders

British Library Cataloguing in Publication Data for this book are
available from the British Library

ISBN 1-899762-57-4 (cased edition)
ISBN 1-899762-59-0 (paperbound edition)

First published 2003

Published by Horus Editions Limited,
27 Longford Street, London NW1 3DZ

Printed in Singpaore

CONTENTS

THE PLANET OF LIFE

HUMANS HAVE explored the farthest corners of planet Earth, and beyond. The greater the distances travelled by spacecraft, and the more we discover about our neighbouring planets, the more unique our own planet seems. We live on an oasis in a vast, empty desert of lifeless planets, circled by lifeless moons, set within the emptiness of lifeless space itself. This oasis planet is fixed in a stable orbit around the star we call the Sun, at a distance that sustains a range of temperatures in which water largely remains a liquid. Wherever there is water on planet Earth there is life.

When we arrive, newborn, in this incredible living world, it is difficult to understand just how old it is. We assume that everything we see has always been there. The 'spiral of life' shows, alongside the date when they first emerged, those animals and plants that have survived into modern times. Generation after generation, the starfish that lived 500 million years ago would be recognised on a beach today. Yet there are also many types of plants and animals that once flourished on the Earth, but that died out long ago. The only reminders of these extinct life forms are the fossils they left behind.

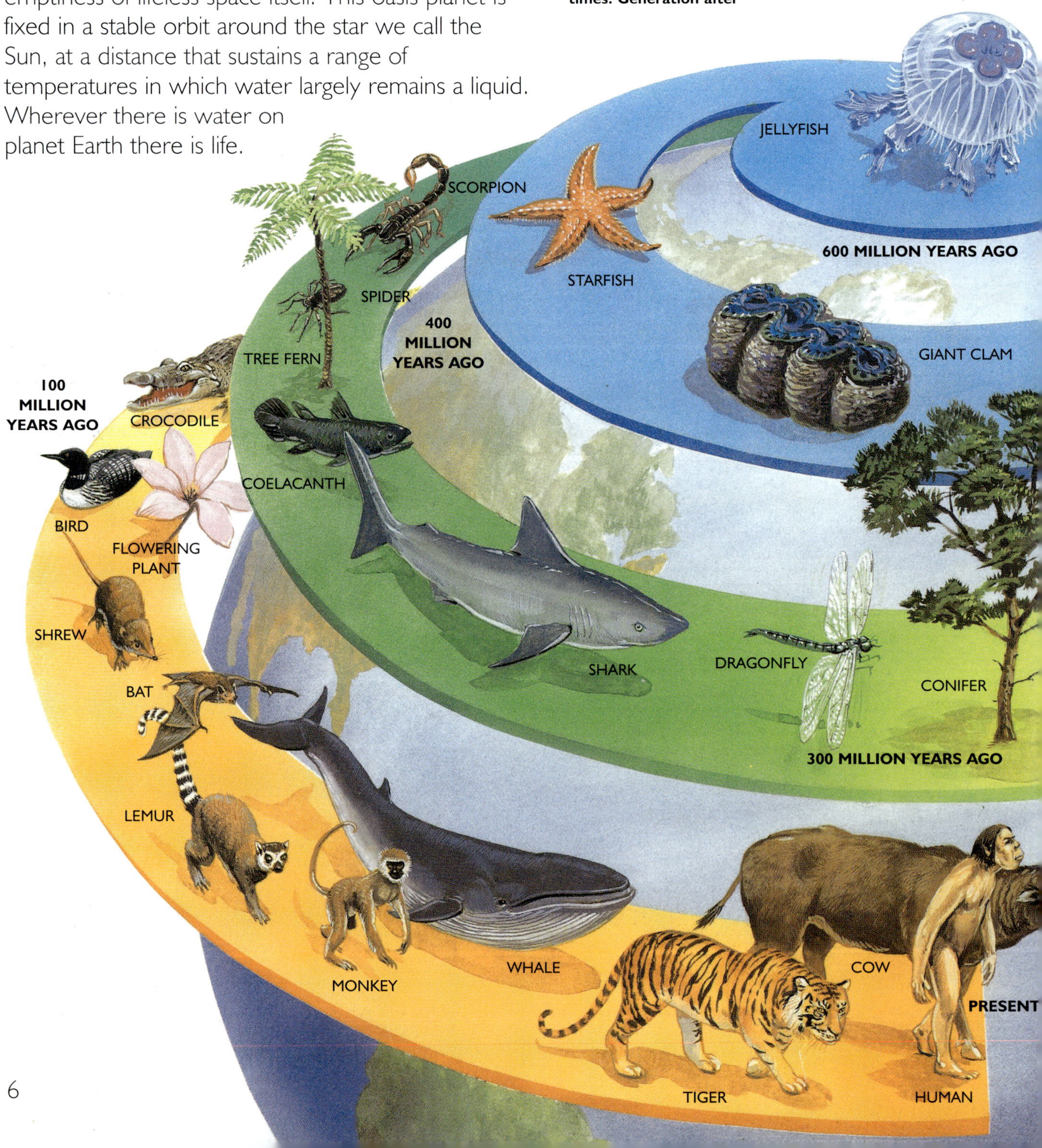

The spiral of life

Earth is like a carriage on a train moving through time. It has picked up animals and plants at different stops, and they all now share each other's company. It is only by travelling back into the past that we can find out when all the different types of animal and plant first appeared on the Earth. Such a journey will also reveal, millions or even billions of years ago, how it is that all animals and plants are distant relatives of one another.

Even some of the most familiar animals and plants alive today illustrate the remarkable history of life on Earth. Some animals, like the strange knobbly crocodile, have changed little in 200 million years. Others, like the tree fern which is more than 300 million years old, seem primitive and ancient. In contrast, delicate flowers have only been in existence for around 100 million years, while animals with fur are even newer.

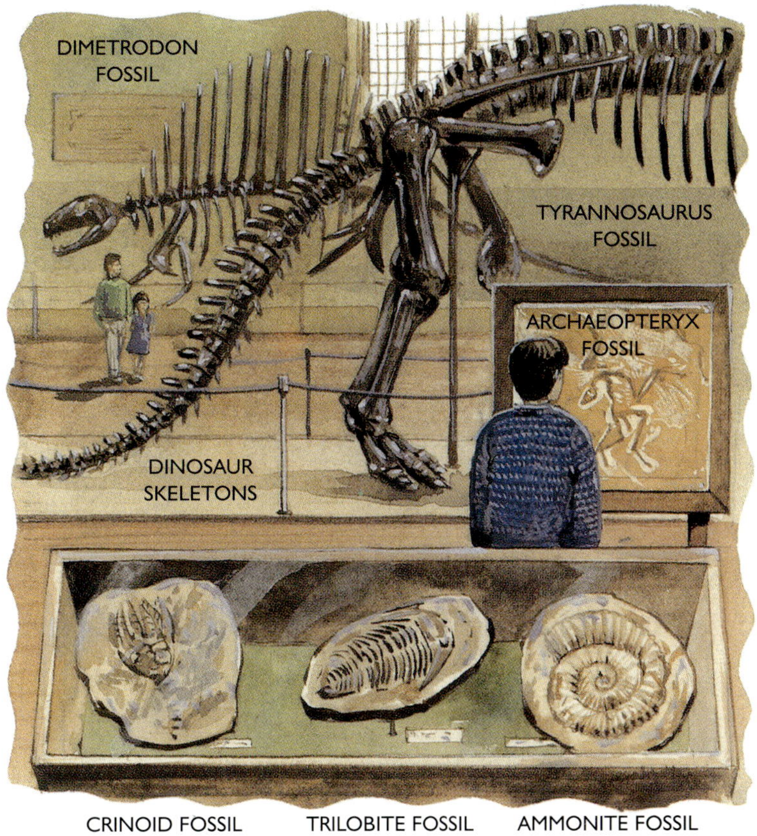

When we visit a museum of prehistoric animals, we come face to face with many types of animal that died out long ago and have no living survivors. Some, like the trilobite that vanished 300 million years ago, are simple in structure but with no modern equivalent; some, like the ammonite, are recognisable but far larger than similar creatures found today. Other fossils can be enormous, such as the bones of the dinosaurs, bigger than any land animal alive. Yet the Earth itself is a living museum housing 10 million types of animal and plant, some of which were first created millions of years ago.

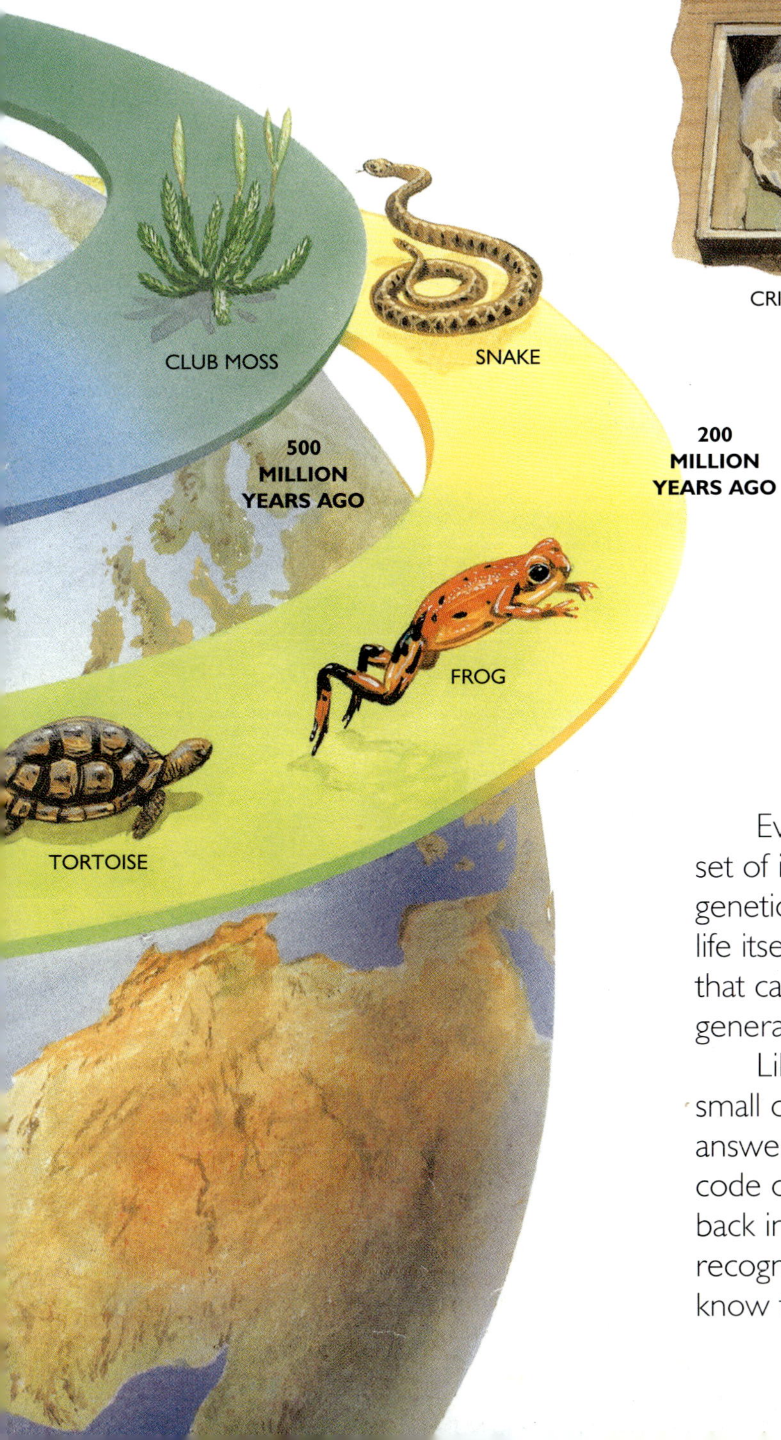

Every living thing grew according to a recipe, a set of instructions known as the 'genetic code'. The genetic code is written into the smallest particle of life itself: the living cell. The cell is the messenger that carries the recipe, and passes it on from one generation to the next, down through time.

Like recipes, the genetic code may undergo small changes through time. As a result, the simplest answer to the question, 'How old is the genetic code of an ostrich, or a panda?' is to say how far back in time an ancestor can be traced that is recognisably similar to the ostrich or panda we know today.

'DEEP TIME'

IT IS VIRTUALLY impossible for us to understand the immense amount of time that has passed since the formation of the Earth. In fact the history of the Earth is so long that we cannot hope to imagine it in our everyday idea of time, or measure it in days, weeks and months. Through history we learn about events, and can visit monuments and old buildings, hundreds of years old. Yet the rocks from which a stone building is constructed may be a million times older than the building itself. Our calendar sets the clock at zero only 2,000 years ago. Yet 2,000 years are no more than an instant in the great journey of the Earth from its birth until today. If the history of the Earth was viewed as a day, 2,000 years would be no more than a twentieth of a second. To understand the beginnings, or origin, of the Earth we need to expand our everyday time into 'deep time', measured in thousands of thousands of thousands (or billions) of years.

Geological time is divided into eras, periods and epochs. These lengths of time were named more than 100 years ago. The names were given to the rocks formed during each period.

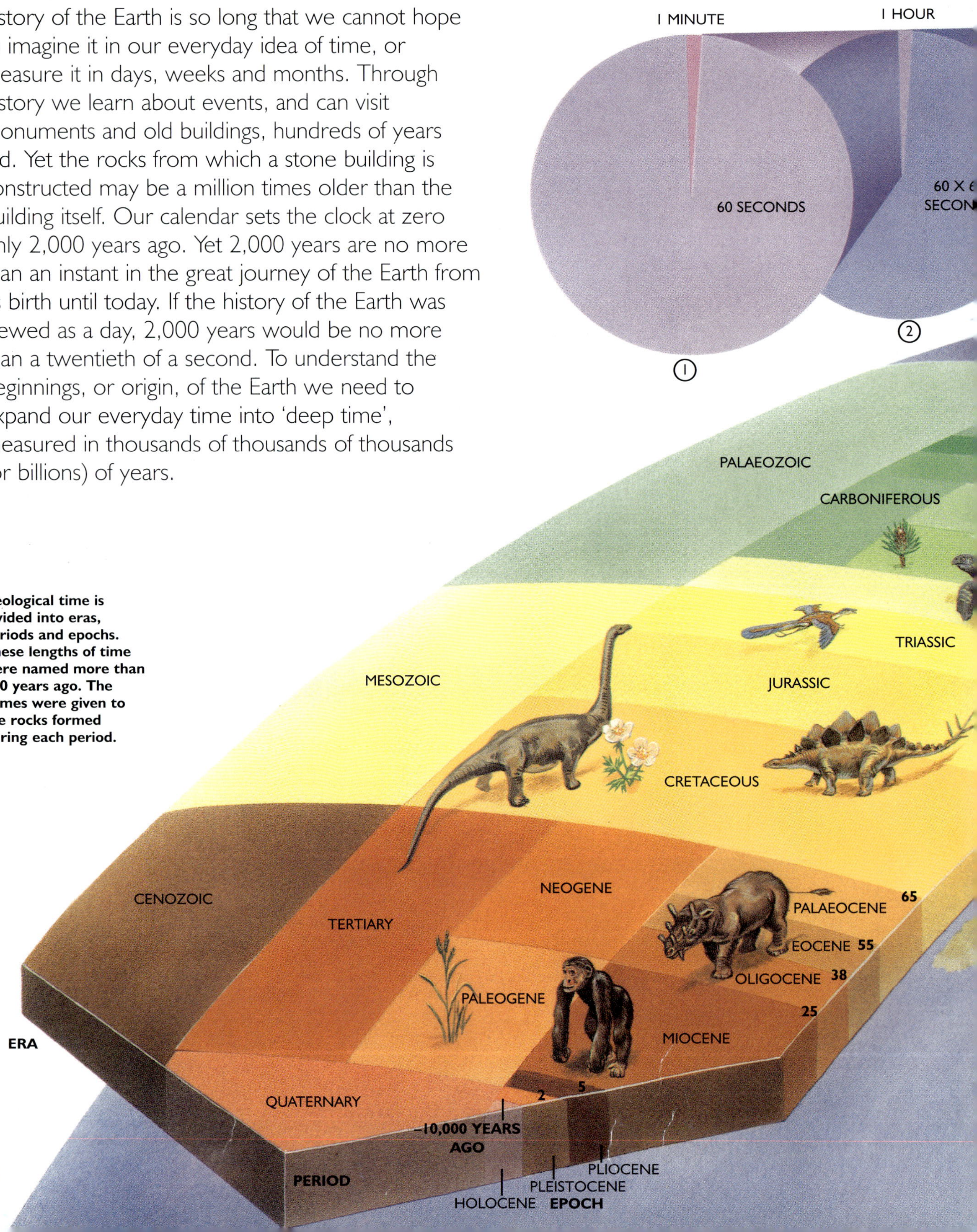

Measuring 'deep time'
Imagine a series of ten dials like those below. The first dial on the left is marking seconds; the one next to it minutes. The hand on each dial must rotate 60 times before the dial to the right turns once. To count the age of the Earth we need all ten dials. The tenth dial would take more than 19 billion years to make a turn, about the age of the Universe, and about four times the age of the Earth.

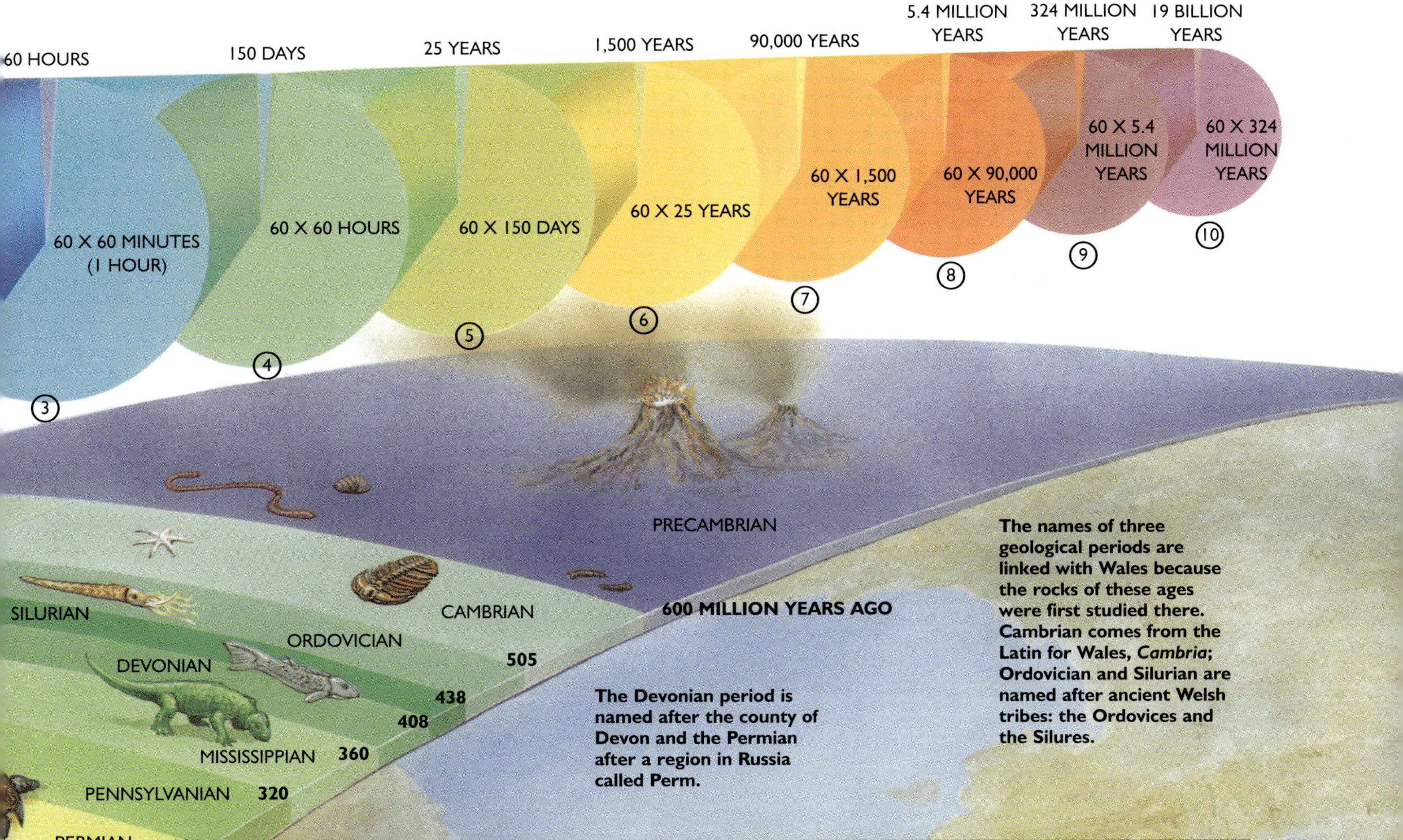

The names of three geological periods are linked with Wales because the rocks of these ages were first studied there. Cambrian comes from the Latin for Wales, *Cambria*; Ordovician and Silurian are named after ancient Welsh tribes: the Ordovices and the Silures.

The Devonian period is named after the county of Devon and the Permian after a region in Russia called Perm.

In France it was thought (mistakenly) that the same type of rock was formed everywhere on Earth at the same time.

The name Carboniferous was given to the 'age of carbon'; the name Cretaceous came from *cretaceus*, a Latin word linked with chalk.

IN TIME, A HUGE CRAGGY ROCK WILL WEAR AWAY TO BECOME A SMOOTH PEBBLE

Understanding 'deep time'
How can we try to understand 'deep time'? When snow melts and disappears, a whole landscape is transformed as it loses its blanket of white. Now imagine that the rocky mountaintops and cliffs are melting and disappearing, just like snow. Over millions of years no mountain is too great to be washed away into the sea; no coastal sea too deep to be filled with vast layers of sediment. The world of rock, which seems so strong and permanent, is actually continuously wearing away.

A WORLD IN CHANGE

The moving continents
Changes to the Earth's surface are caused by movements of white-hot rocks deep within the planet. This movement drags sections of the outer shell, known as plates, at speeds of a few centimetres each year. Most earthquakes occur along the edges of the plates. In the past 160 million years, a line of deep cracks has slowly widened to form the Atlantic Ocean, while the Indian Ocean has appeared where the southern continents have spun away from one another. Another ocean, called Tethys, that once separated Africa and India from Asia, has been swallowed by the Earth.

THE MAP of the world seems fixed, yet nothing about the Earth is permanent. Land is being worn away by rivers and the sea, submerged by earthquakes, and destroyed by volcanoes. At the same time, new land is born: new sandbanks and river deltas, new islands and new mountains. Even the continents are not fixed in place. One hundred million years ago, dinosaurs could walk on dry land from London to New York.

The city of Atlantis is supposed to have disappeared almost 3,000 years ago. It is said that, in a night of floods and earthquakes, it vanished beneath the sea. The story of Atlantis is thought to be about the destruction of the Minoan civilisation in Crete, an island in the eastern Mediterranean Sea.

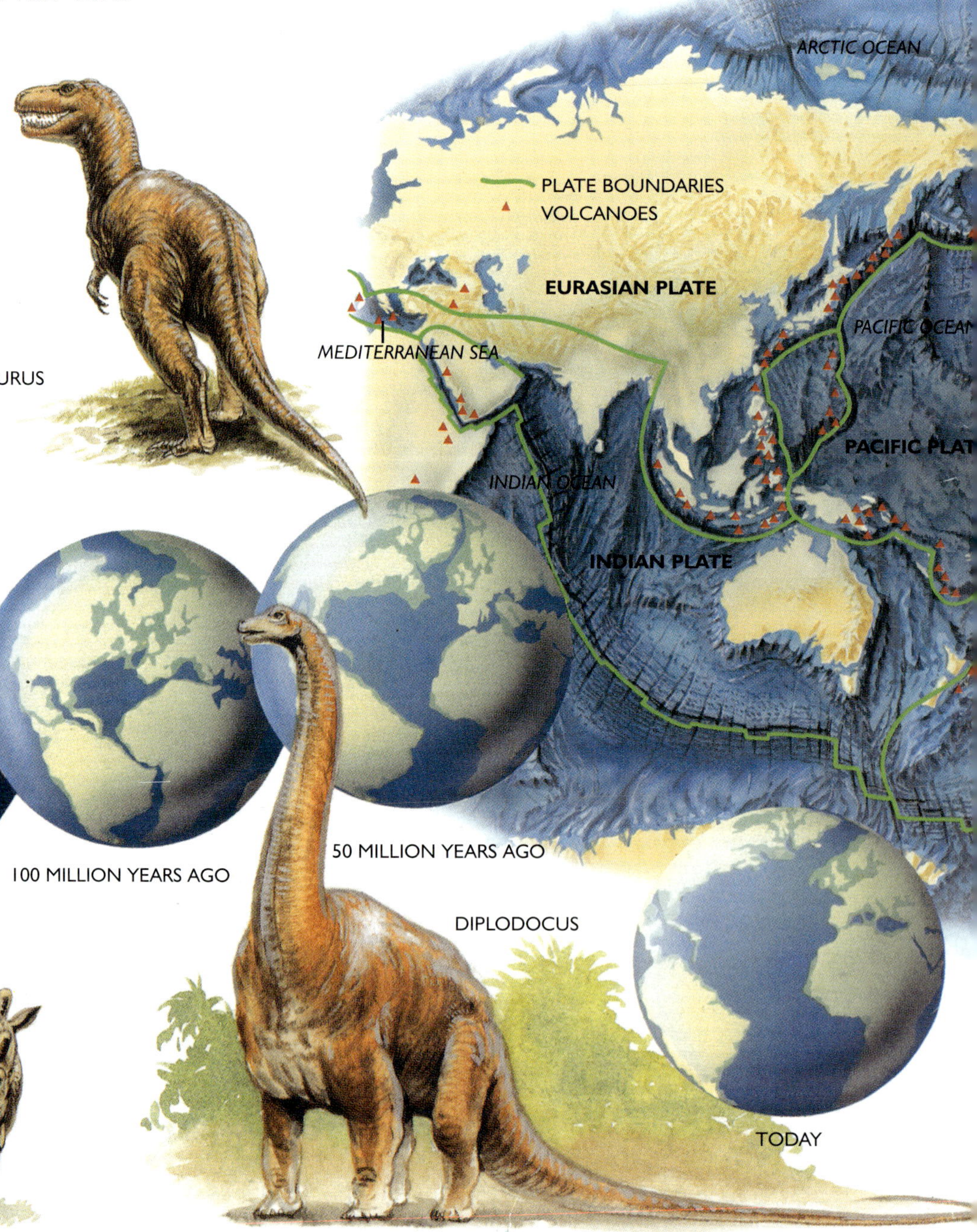

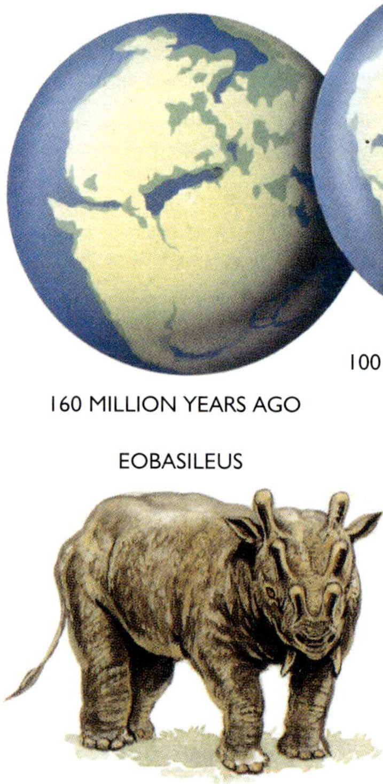

Seven thousand years ago, the level of the sea was rising as fast as 5 cm every year. The oceans were filling up with water from the gigantic melting ice caps that had once covered the whole of northern Europe and northern North America. Many areas of dry land, such as those that once connected North America to Asia or Britain to Europe, had become covered with water. As the sea level changed, so animals and plants had to adapt to a new landscape.

Destruction and creation
Volcanic eruptions, like the explosion that pulverised the Indonesian island of Krakatoa in 1883, can be the most devastating events on Earth. Yet volcanoes can also create new land. In November 1963, a new island was born in the Atlantic Ocean, to the south-west of Iceland. It was created by an underwater volcanic eruption. In 18 months, the new island of Surtsey grew 200 m high, and more than 1 km long.

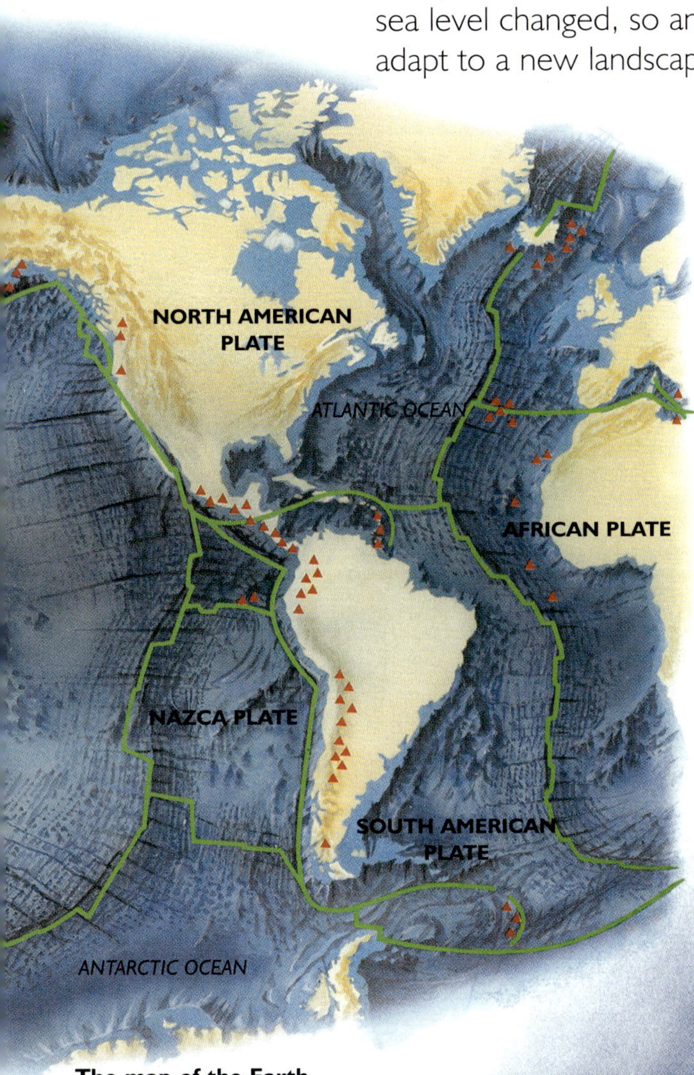

The map of the Earth
All around the Pacific Ocean the ocean floor is being eaten away by the surrounding continents. In contrast, the great Atlantic Ocean continues to widen. Stretching from Spain to China, a chain of mountains continues to grow as the southern landmasses slowly collide with Asia.

Life on Earth
The moving continents have slowly separated populations of animals and plants by thousands of miles and this has had an immense impact on the evolution of life. Some animals and plants evolved into distinct new species, while many species became extinct. In the time of the supercontinent Pangaea, dinosaurs ruled the Earth. Later, the animals living in Australia or South America became quite different from those of Europe or North America. Today, the largest animals, the whales, live in the sea.

THE YOUNG EARTH

THE EARTH was born 4.6 billion years ago, at the same time as all the other planets, rocky asteroids and icy comets that, together with the Sun, make up the Solar System. Everything in our Solar System, even the plants and animals on Earth, was created from the remains of an exploded star. Each of the planets and their moons formed out of the resulting swirling cloud of gas and dust. Much of the material in this cloud collapsed to form the Sun, but the outer disc settled into rings and later into great masses of rock and gas: the planets.

The inner planets – Mercury, Venus, Earth and Mars – have only thin atmospheres because the Sun's fierce rays blasted other gas away. Further from the Sun, the enormous outer planets – Jupiter, Saturn and Neptune – are largely made up of gas. The Moon split from the Earth very soon after the planets began to form.

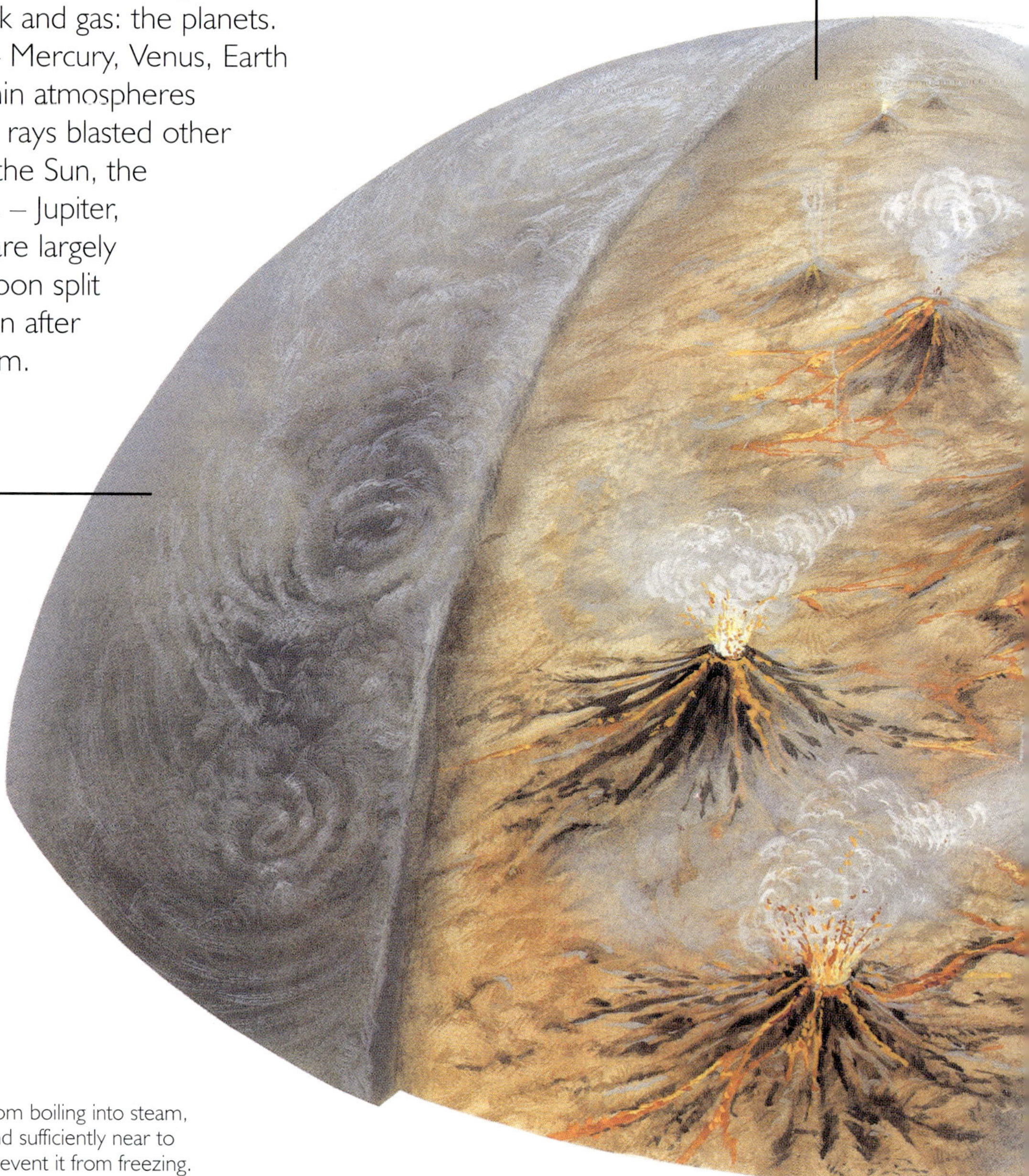

From chaos to life
Having lost its first atmosphere, the Earth became a barren planet, peppered with volcanoes. The gas that erupted from these volcanoes helped to create a new atmosphere rich in nitrogen, carbon and water vapour. This atmosphere kept the surface of the Earth warm. One day, for the first time, it rained: a rain rich in acids. Soon streams ran into pools and the pools expanded into seas and oceans. The Earth was far enough from the Sun to prevent the water from boiling into steam, and sufficiently near to prevent it from freezing. Earth had become the water planet, and out of this water came life.

The origin of life

THE first life existed around four billion years ago. These primitive life-forms were simply a series of chemicals arranged in a long chain that had the ability to make copies of themselves.

We know that all life on Earth has come ultimately from the same parent because deep within the cells of all plants and animals lies the same code for life: an identical pattern of chemicals that tells every animal and plant how to grow *(see page 15)*.

Old rocks

Some meteorites are fragments of a planet that once lay between Mars and Jupiter, and orbit the Sun as thousands of rocky asteroids. Other meteorites are the remains of the original material of the Solar System. Rocks from the Moon are younger (4.35 billion years old). The Moon itself broke off from the Earth after a collision with a planet-sized asteroid.

THE FIRST RAINS

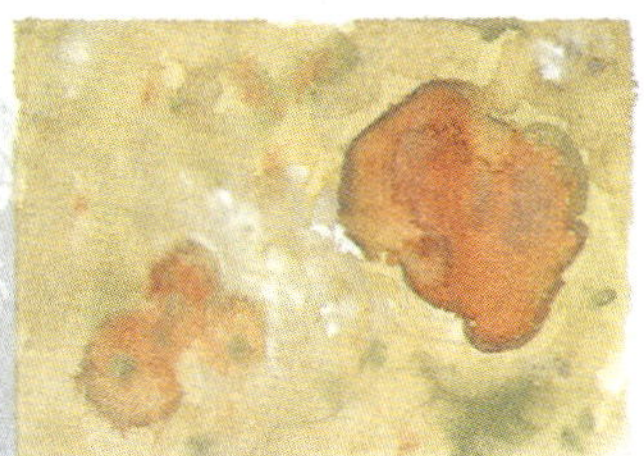

Some bacteria grow in volcanic pools because volcanoes produce lots of hydrogen sulphide (a gas), from which bacteria extract hydrogen to make their food.

The oldest fossils

Over a long period of time primitive bacteria developed a chemistry that allowed them to extract hydrogen from water while releasing oxygen – a process known as 'photosynthesis'. These bacteria, called 'blue-greens' (or *cyanophytes*), spread into ponds, rivers and seas. Where the water that they lived in was limey, the blue-greens extracted the water and left the lime as a hard scale that developed into pillow-size mats, called stromatolites.

Stromatolites are some of the oldest-known fossils (2.8 billion years old) and are found in many places. Living stromatolites can still be seen in a few places today, such as in parts of Australia and Indonesia.

By extracting hydrogen from water and releasing oxygen into the air, the blue-greens gradually changed the chemistry of the Earth's atmosphere, increasing the level of oxygen to one-fifth of the atmosphere.

AUSTRALIAN STROMATOLITES

EVOLUTION

Taller or smaller
Evolution occurs because particular environments favour the survival of individuals with certain characteristics. Where these environments change, the animals and plants may have to evolve to continue to thrive in them. This environmental change may come from a variation in the climate, from increased competition for food, the arrival of a new predator, or from the movement of the animal or plant to a new place. Imagine a country in which an increasing number of animals want the food on the lower branches of trees and you can see how evolution favoured animals with long necks and how, over many generations, giraffes became taller so as to reach the tallest branches.

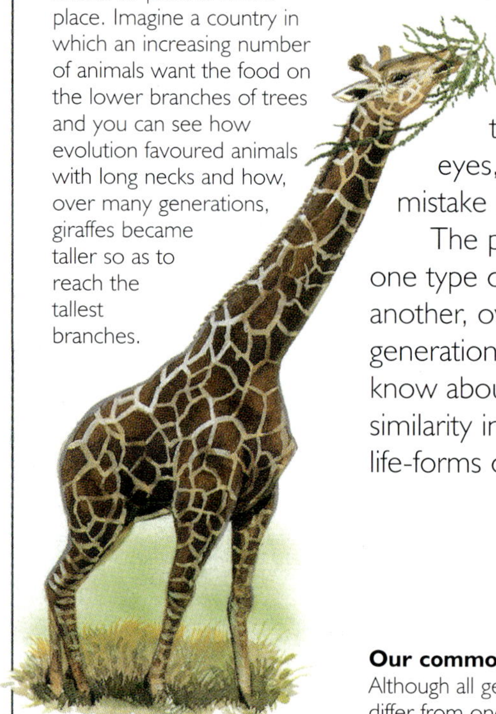

IN ALL BUT the most primitive organisms, the instructions from which the child has grown, called the 'genetic code', are a mixture from both parents. (The genetic code is the set of instructions that exists in every living cell, which instructs the animal how to grow and how to live.) A brother and sister have codes constructed from a mixture of their mother's and father's codes, but the pieces will have come together slightly differently. There are so many possibilities that every animal's code is unique.

The genetic code is so long and complex that changes can occur spontaneously. Such changes often do not improve an animal's chances of survival, but sometimes such mistakes can help the animal. Jaws, ears, fins, hands, even eyes, probably all began with a chance mistake in the genetic code.

The process of change of one type of animal or plant into another, over numerous generations, is called 'evolution'. We know about evolution because of the similarity in the genetic codes of all the life-forms on Earth.

Some characteristics can help an animal to survive long enough to have offspring. Genes carried by successful animals will become more widespread than genes carried by animals that did not survive for long enough to breed.

TYRANNOSAURUS ATTACKS TRICERATOPS' ANCESTORS

TRICERATOPS DEVELOPS BETTER DEFENCES

Our common ancestor
Although all genetic codes differ from one another, they have much in common. The similarity between the codes of a human and a chimpanzee is closer than the similarity between the codes of a human and a cat, and far closer than the similarity between a human and a snake. The closer the genetic codes of two species of animal, the more recently they possessed a common ancestor.

The ancestors of *Triceratops* were easily attacked and killed by the terrible *Tyrannosaurus*. Over time *Triceratops* became bigger, also developing larger and sharper horns. Eventually, *Triceratops* were able to stand up to their attackers.

Once, people saw evolution as no more than competition; a world in which the strongest always did best and the weak were crushed. Yet the very opposite of competition – one animal helping another – is also of great importance. A baby is dependent on its mother, a sick animal on one that is well, an old animal on one that is young. Many animals, just like humans, live in societies in which the survival and health of the individual is dependent on the health of the whole community.

Animals that help and support one another may have a better chance of passing on their genes than those that do not. The communities that help one another are often closely interrelated, meaning that they share very similar genes. The help these relatives give one another allows the community to bring up more children, and this in turn ensures that these genes are passed on to more individuals in the next generation.

TRICERATOPS DEFENDS ITSELF AGAINST TYRANNOSAURUS

Some of the most communal animals are the ants and bees, who devote all their energies to their queen and her eggs.

The book of life

At the heart of every cell lies the same twisted strand of millions of simple chemicals, known as DNA. DNA is organised into a highly complex 'book' of instructions: the genetic code. Individual genes tell cells how to build complete plants or animals.

When the remains of living creatures were found in rocks known to be about 550 million years old, people thought that this was the time when life had actually begun. We now know that life had been continuing for around 3 billion years before then. What we can see in the rocks is evidence of the time when animals first discovered how to use chemicals dissolved in sea water to build hard rocky parts around their bodies. These rocky parts survived after the animal had died, and it is these 'fossils' that we see in the rocks today.

The Burgess Shale

BECAUSE of the way that a mudslide suddenly poured into a shallow lagoon 520 million years ago, many of the Burgess Shale fossils are of animals with soft bodies, very rarely preserved in rocks. The fossil record of life usually presents a one-sided view: we know a lot about animals with hard shells and bones, but almost nothing of those with only soft tissues. However, the Burgess Shale has preserved a complete picture of the whole range of animals alive in the sea at this unusual time. Some animals look relatively familiar, including the sponges, trilobites, worms, sea urchins and shellfish. Others look as

Jellyfish and sea pens
Jellyfish release eggs that grow into tiny bud-like organisms that cling to the seafloor, known as polyps. In another adaptation the polyps stay stuck to the rocks as sea anemones or leaf-like sea pens. Other polyps form colonies that build fantastic rocky coral sculptures.

though they are from science fiction, with no known descendants.

Among these freaks there was *Opabinia*, with a 10-cm long body covered with flaps, a large tail-fan, a head with five eyes, and a set of teeth located at the end of a flexible neck. *Wiwaxia* was like a slug but covered with spines and scales. Most extraordinary was *Hallucigenia*. It seems to have moved on seven pairs of spiny stilt-legs, and grabbed its food with seven tentacles each armed with snappers like those on a crab's claw.

In 1909 an American explorer, Charles Doolittle Walcott, made a remarkable discovery in the Canadian Rockies. While travelling through the Burgess mountain pass he found fossils over 520 million years old. During the years that followed, he collected thousands of them.

About 1.2 billion years ago, some of the simplest life-forms became mixed up together inside a single cell, known as a *protistan*. This cell contained one part that was able to burn oxygen for energy and another part that could build a beating tail. Between one billion and 800 million years ago, these tiny single-cell animals began to grow together in clusters, and to surround themselves with a tough flexible material known as a sponge. In the next stage of evolution, these individual cells combined themselves into single large bodies. Different parts of these bodies had different functions. Jellyfish were some of the first of these many-celled creatures. They had cells that worked as muscles and cells that combined to make a nervous system and cells that made up poisonous weapons for self-defence.

Building for protection

ALGAE and sponges were the first life-forms to learn to build with rock for protection. The structures that they built were haphazard, and it was not until animals discovered how to order the crystals of limestone in precise shapes that they succeeded in mastering their material. This was a major breakthrough in the evolution of life. Animals that could hide in shells or armour were protected. Their attackers had to grow bigger, faster, stronger and brighter in order to continue to feed. This, in turn, encouraged the defenders to protect themselves more, and so it has always continued.

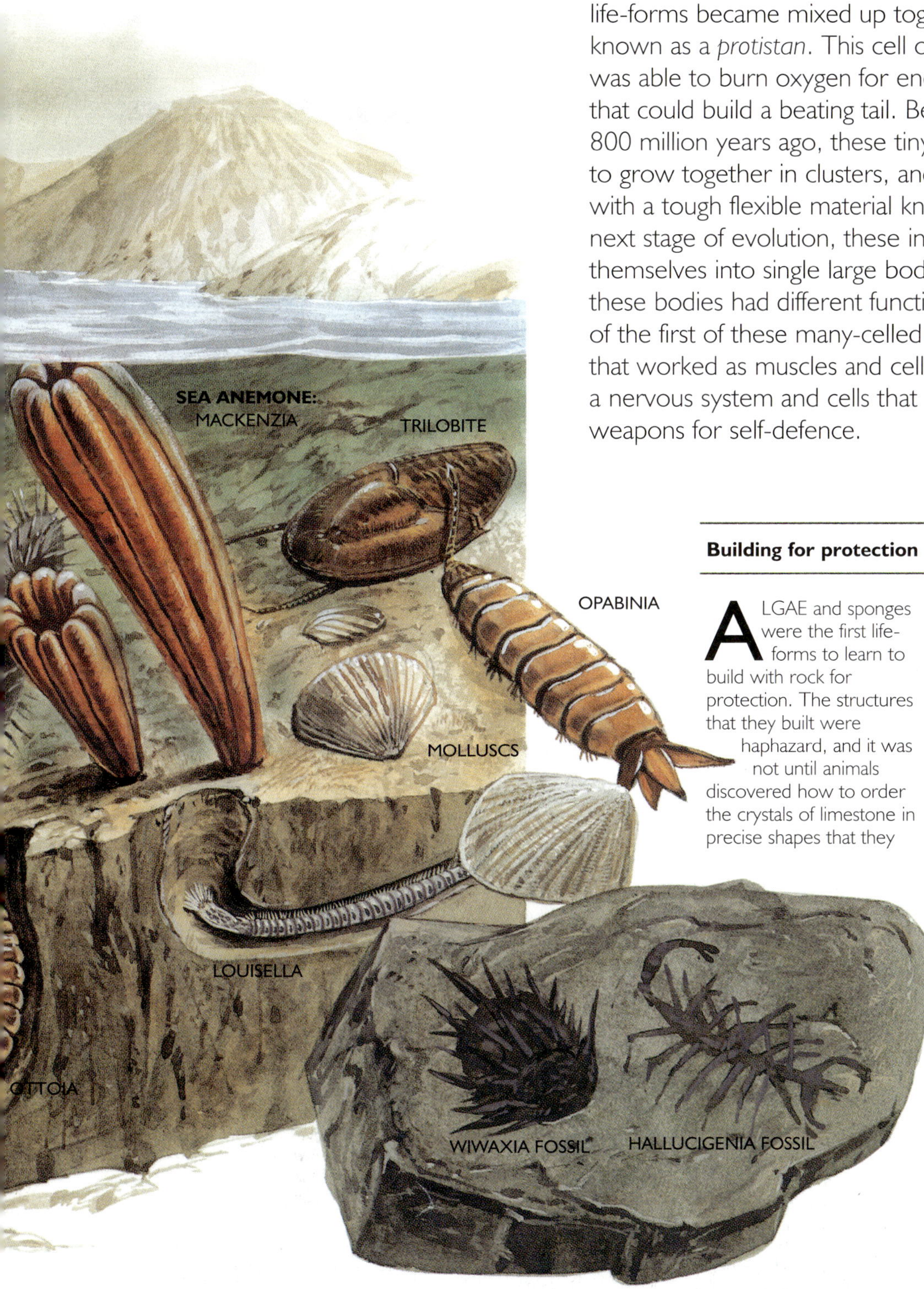

The Burgess Shale fossils are some of the most perfectly preserved in the world. *Wiwaxia* and *Hallucigenia* were two of the creatures fossilised there.

THE RECORD IN THE STONE

WE WOULD know almost nothing about the history of life on Earth if it were not for fossils. Shells on a beach are usually washed or blown away, lost forever. When preserved by chance in drifts of volcanic ash or mud, they become fossils. As fossils they provide occasional snapshots of the history of life.

Usually the soft-bodied parts of an animal decay rapidly on death, leaving behind only the hard parts to be fossilised, such as shells, coral skeletons, animal bones, shark's teeth, the armour of a trilobite.

Only very occasionally are the soft parts of

Trace fossils
Trace fossils are not evidence of the animals' themselves. Instead, they are signs of how the animals lived. The most common trace fossils are the burrows

made by worms and molluscs in the sands and muds of the seafloor. Other trace fossils are the surface marks left by animals creeping and crawling – grooves, paths and trails.

Fossilisation
Many fossils have survived only because of sudden and great changes in the environment in the past, causing the animals and plants to be buried.

Animals in the sea are much more likely to end up as fossils than those on the land, because the surface of the land is constantly being worn away. Fossils of bones or shells often become

1. The dead animal lies in the soft sand and mud of the seabed.

2. Minerals from the mud gradually replace the material of the bones.

More trace fossils
A leaf falling into the mud of a pond is familiar enough in autumn. However, few of these leaf prints will turn into fossils. Some of the most exciting trace fossils are the footprints of animals on an ancient beach or riverbed.

A LEAF FOSSIL IN COAL

DINOSAUR FOOTPRINTS

INSECT PRESERVED IN AMBER

flattened as the mud or sand that surrounds them is squeezed by the weight of the deposits above. Only if the material of the bones or shells is replaced and hardened by minerals in the soil or sea soon after burial will they keep their shape. After millions of years, the fossil bones of an ancient fish-lizard might reappear in the rocks of a cliff.

animals turned into fossils. There are some rare fossils of animals with no hard parts at all, such as worms and jellyfish *(see pages 16–17)*. When the soft parts of animals are preserved it is often after a sudden catastrophe, like an underwater landslide or an erupting volcano. If the sea-floor is rapidly covered with a thick layer of fine mud, soft tissues are protected from the oxygen and micro-organisms that would destroy them. The soft tissues of land animals are only fossilised when the living animal has fallen into a deep bog, or into tarpits where natural crude oil escapes to the surface.

The youngest fossils
Fossil humans, thousands of years old, have been found in the peat bogs of northern Europe. Their skins have been pickled to leather. Other fossil humans have been found thawing out of glaciers.

The youngest fossils are found in the Pacific Ocean, where coral animals have built reefs around skeletons of soldiers killed in World War II, sunken ships, and even fizzy-drink bottles.

The area that was a is now marshy amp. The fossil lies ep below the rface.

4. The sea erodes land to form a new cliff.

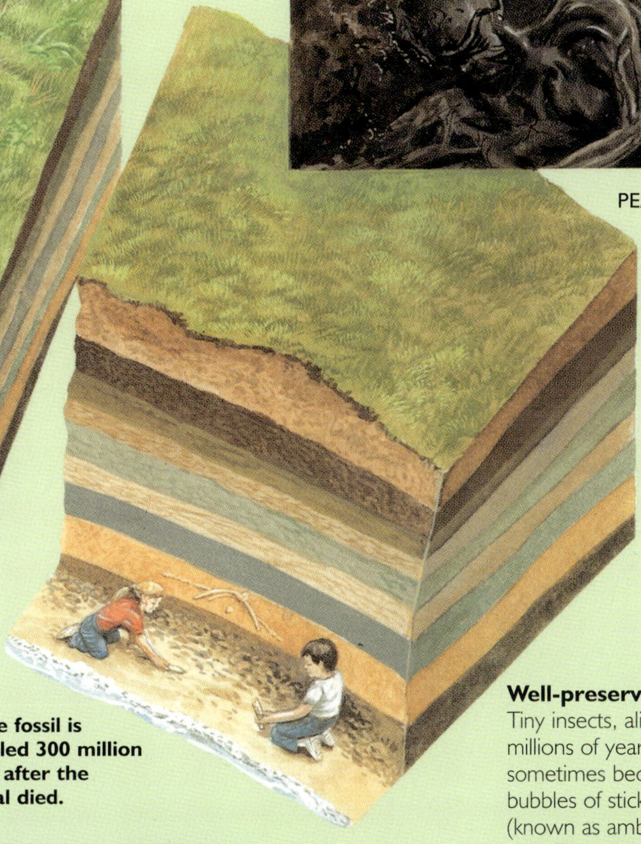

5. The fossil is revealed 300 million years after the animal died.

PEAT-BOG MAN

Well-preserved fossils
Tiny insects, alive many millions of years ago, have sometimes become stuck in bubbles of sticky resin (known as amber) from a tree. They are often perfectly preserved. In the frozen ground (or permafrost) of northern Asia, Ice Age animals have been deep-frozen for thousands of years. These animals, such as mammoths, have been carefully dug out to be examined and displayed in museums.

FOSSILS IN STONE

DEEP-FROZEN BABY MAMMOTH

The flat, spiralled shells of the ammonites first appeared around 500 million years ago. Ammonites could float and may have been blown across the water by the wind. Some were as large as cart wheels.

All the varieties of animals alive in the seas between 550 and 500 million years ago can be divided into three basic groups: those that lived in shells, those that had a five-pointed star form, and those that had bodies divided into segments. Each of these three designs was well adapted to life in the seas, and each evolved into many variations that continue, even today, to make up a major part of the living world.

Many of the huge variety of animals that evolved in the seas in prehistoric times still survive

Shells of all shapes

SHELLS are built by a line or curve of cells that secrete a regular layer of calcium carbonate crystals, as the animal inside expands. The geometry of the shell reflects the way in which the shape has stayed the same even as the shell has continued to grow – in some organisms as a simple curved covering, in others as a spiral disc or turret.

The first shells were grown by primitive flatworms that burrowed into the sand. Some of the oldest of these shellfish, known as *Lingulella*, have scarcely changed, and can still be found in the sea today (called *Lingula*). Shells with two halves are generally found on animals that clamp themselves with a strong foot to the seafloor, while single-shelled molluscs can move about freely.

BRACHIOPOD SHELL ROOTED TO THE SEA BED

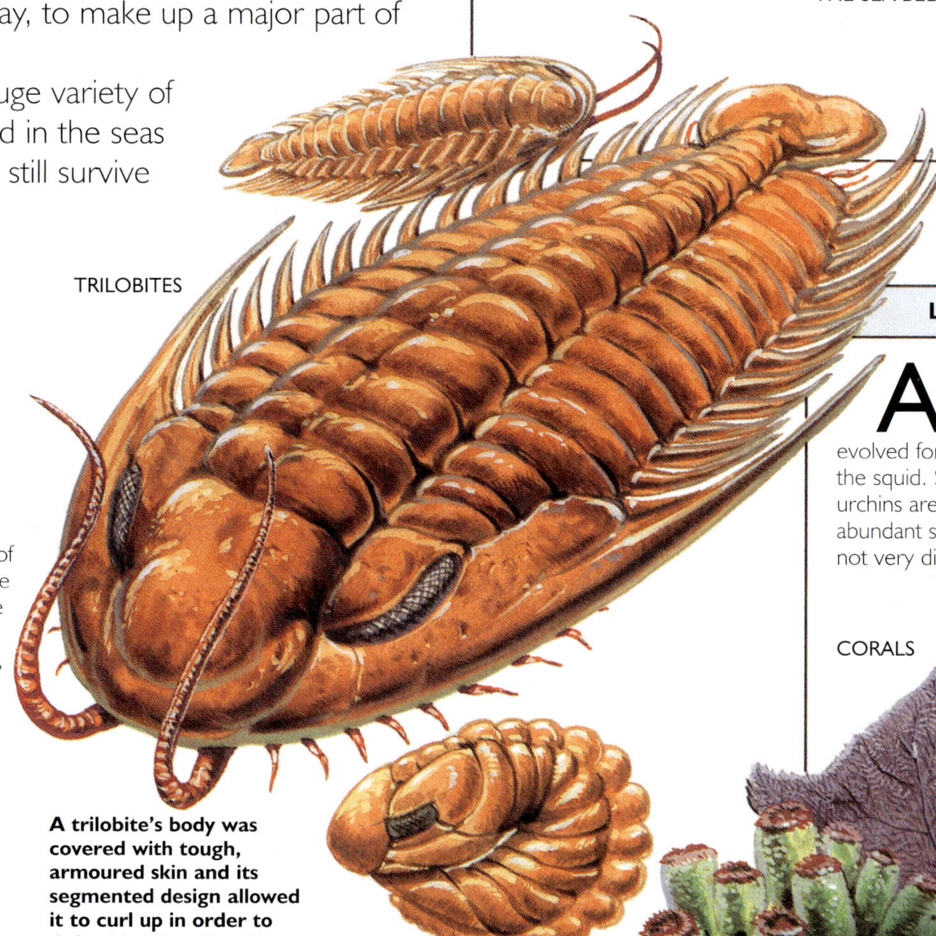

TRILOBITES

The trilobites

Animals with bodies made of segments were to prove the most successful of the three groups. The segmented body could have many legs, claws or antennae. Each segment also gained the ability to grow a section of interlocking shell. The first animals with these adaptations were the trilobites, creatures that looked like giant wood lice. Between 500 and 400 million years ago they scurried across the seafloor, paddled through the water, or swam upside-down at the surface. The largest trilobites were the size of small plates. Another group of segmented animals that appeared around the same time as the trilobites were the crustacea, which includes crabs, lobsters, shrimps and crayfish: all of which, unlike the trilobites, have survived to the present day.

A trilobite's body was covered with tough, armoured skin and its segmented design allowed it to curl up in order to defend itself, rather like a wood louse.

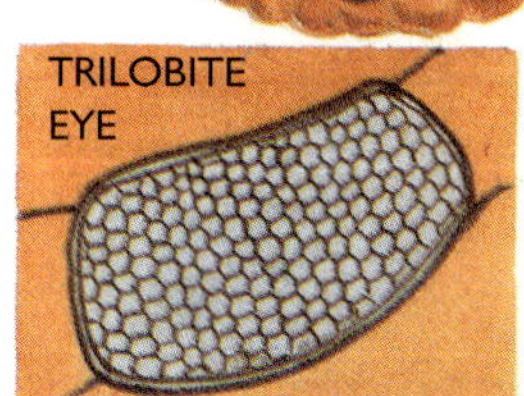

Life in the oceans

ANIMALS with the five-pointed star shape never evolved forms as mobile as the squid. Starfish and sea urchins are the most abundant survivors and are not very different from their

CORALS

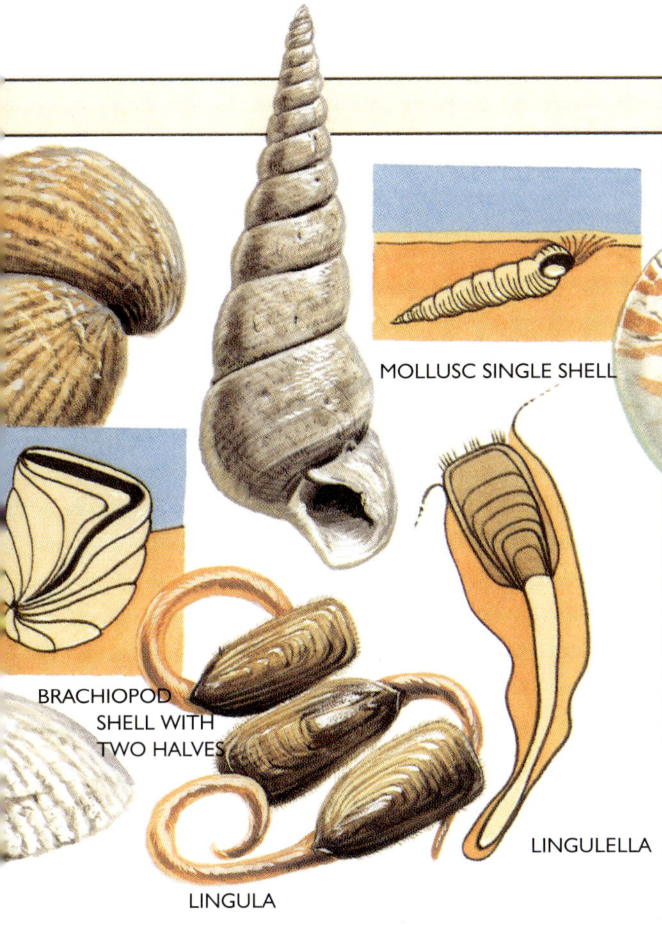

DID YOU KNOW?

The pearly nautilus is the only survivor of the ammonites. Two other varieties lost their shells: the swift squid and the slower octopus.

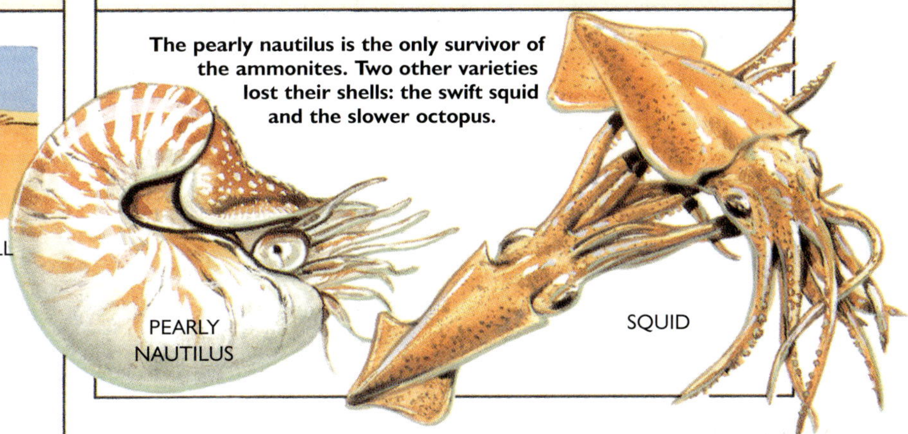

in a similar form in today's seas and oceans. Others that were once successful have died out. Around 400 million years ago, trilobites of all shapes and sizes were some of the most common of all sea-life, found roaming in all the seas. Yet by 250 million years ago, following a world wide catastrophe in which many different marine and land species died out, they had all disappeared.

500-million-year-old relatives. Starfish are very strong, able to pry open large clams as their arms lock onto the shell with suckers.

The most abundant of the star-shaped animals were the crinoids, also known as sea lilies. They had bodies with five arm-like tentacles.

For the past 250 million years primitive animals, known as polyps, have lived in vast colonies: the coral reefs. These reefs reach up to the light at the sea's surface, and provide a rich concentration of life.

Crinoid fossils
Crinoids were very common about 300 million years ago. The largest of the crinoids had stems 20 m long. Only a few crinoids still survive, in the depths of the oceans.

The oldest fish

Arandaspis is one of the oldest-known fossil fish, dating from around 500 million years ago. Only 15 cm long, with no jaws, and covered with thin bony scales, it must have swum like a stiff tadpole.

Of all the creatures that were alive 550 million years ago, one small organism was to be the creator of the most important dynasty in the history of planet Earth. This small creature had the beginnings of a backbone, a thin internal rod. A backbone can support a long streamlined body or it can provide a rigid support against which muscles can pull. Backbones allowed the development of speed, agility, strength and size in the animal world.

Sharks are among the oldest fish with cartilage backbones and skeletons, and were, from the

Fish with jaws

About 425 million years ago, fish began to evolve variations with jaws. Jaws allowed fish to bite and tear, not just filter and suck their food. The fish with jaws divided into two groups. In the first, the bones stayed in the form in which they first appear in the young fish – made out of cartilage, a light flexible material rather like plastic. In the second this cartilage was replaced by harder bone. *Spathobathis*, *Hybodus* and *Sclerorhynchus* are early jawed fish with backbones formed of cartilage.

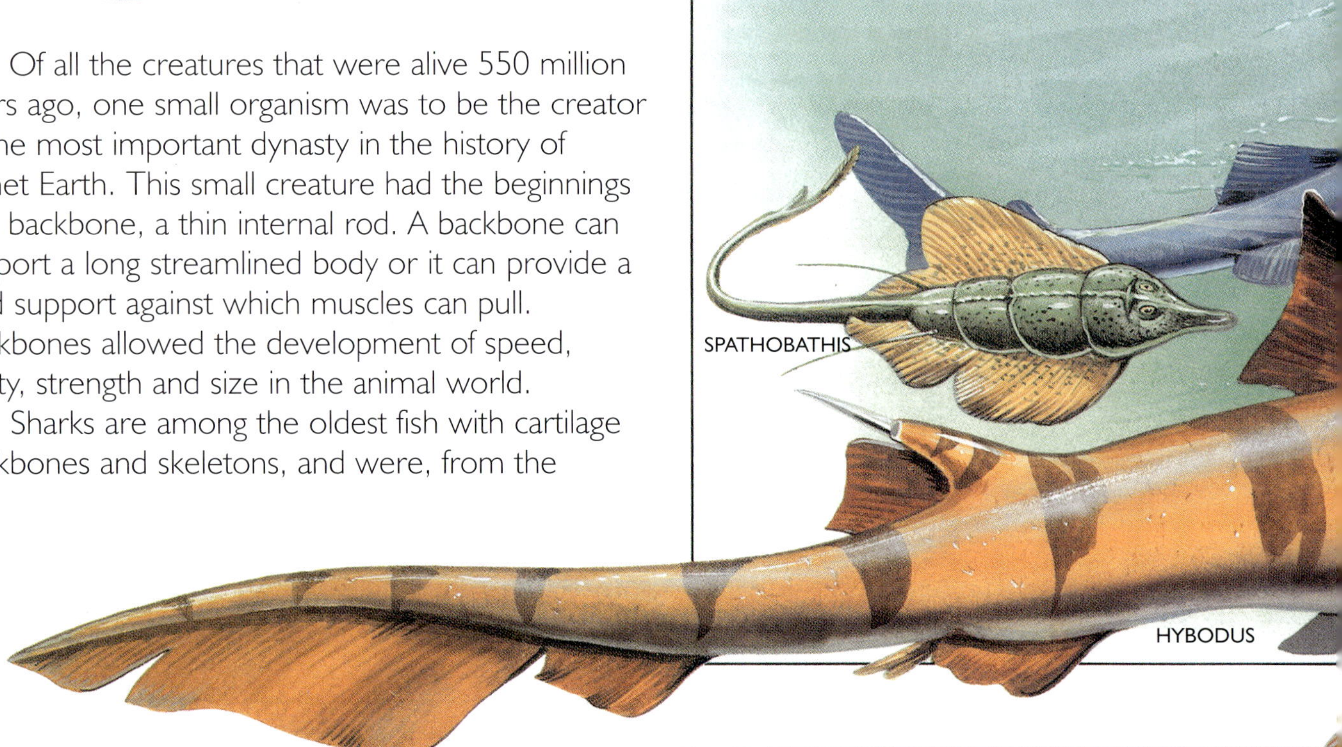

Armoured fish

The one thing that an internal skeleton does not provide is protection against hungry rivals. The fish with backbones were small and slow and, as a result, needed the protection of armour plating.

At the start they hid their bodies in a box of plates and had a flexible tail. They had no fins, so they moved by beating their tails from side to side. Their heavy armoured plates kept them weighed down in the water. Lacking any jaws, they grazed among the debris from other animals on the seabed. Their enemies included the molluscs and jellyfish, as well as the terrifying claws of 2 m-long sea scorpions.

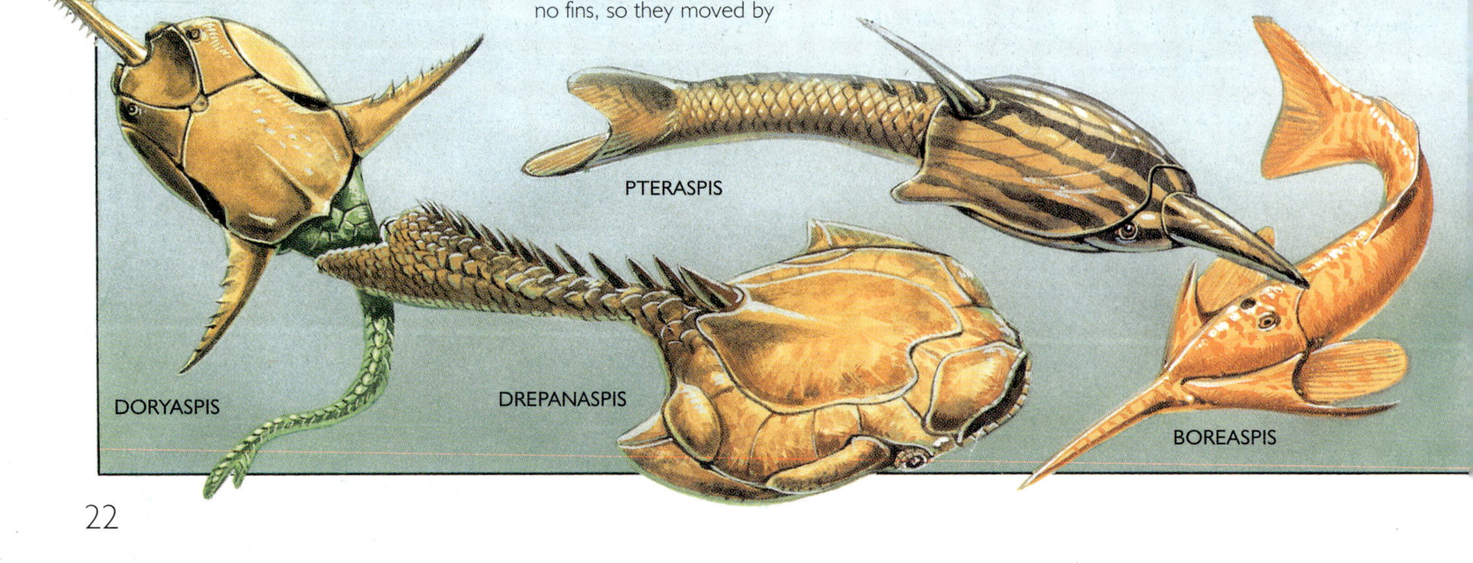

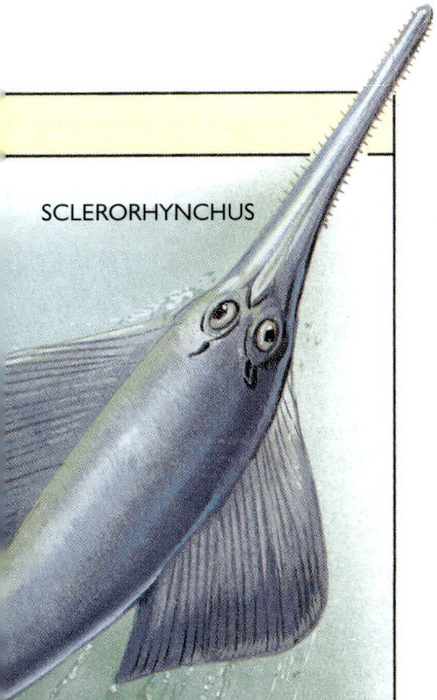

Fishy remains
Fossilised skeletons of bony fish have been found. However, cartilage is softer than bone and rots away. As a result, the only traces of the earliest sharks are their teeth.

beginning, fierce hunters. Their methods of hunting were particularly hard on their teeth, so sharks developed a spiral production line of more than 50 teeth in which new teeth rotated into place as the older ones wore away. Of all the parts of the shark it is only their teeth that become fossilised, and in some marine sediments these teeth, dropped throughout a shark's life, can be very common. Modern sharks first appeared about 100 million years ago.

The bony fish developed vertebrae that interlocked to create a strong and movable spine. Once they acquired jaws, these early fish became the most important ocean hunters, sometimes reaching lengths of 6 or 7 m.

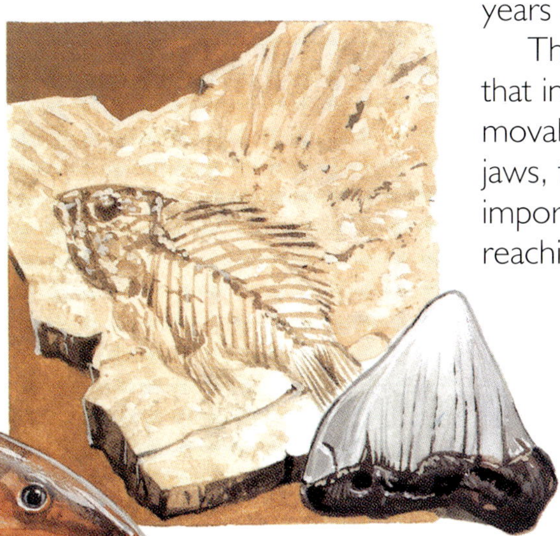

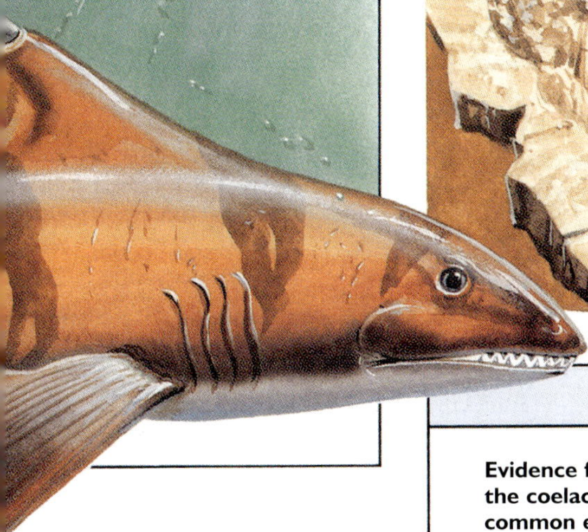

DID YOU KNOW?

Evidence from fossils suggested that the coelacanth, one of the most common early jawed fish, had become extinct about 100 million years ago. Then, in 1938, the captain of a South African trawler fishing in the Indian Ocean had his hand almost bitten off by a fierce fish pulled from the deep. A local biologist, in amazement, recognised it as a coelacanth, a 'living fossil'.

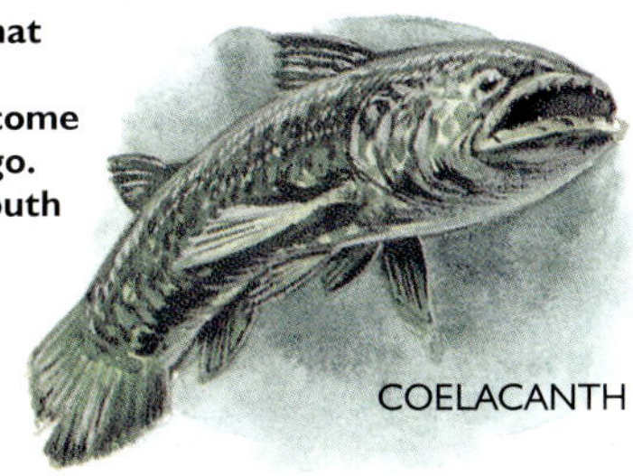

Some modern fish have re-learned the importance of armour. The slow-moving seahorse has a rigid, upright body with fins on each side.

Jawless survivors
Two survivors of the earliest primitive jawless fish are still alive today. The pink eel-like hagfish lives by grasping chunks of flesh from dead fish. The lamprey sucks the flesh and blood of fish with its primitive mouth.

Sharks, skates and rays
Sharks constantly sweep their tails from side to side to stop themselves from sinking. Modern skates and rays have 'wings' and glide through the oceans.

CONQUERING THE LAND

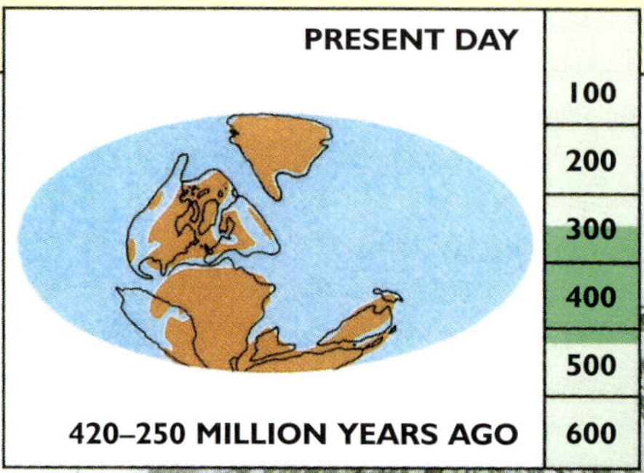

THE GREENING of the land occurred suddenly, around 420 million years ago. For billions of years, slimy algae had lived along the seashore, clinging to the rocks and kept moist by the spray of the waves. Then one patch of algae evolved a waxy skin that protected the cells from drying out in the sun. These waxy coverings enclosing the green cells became the first plants. With this simple protection the plants began to invade the land, first concentrating in areas around swamps and river banks. Descendants of these early plants are still alive today.

A barren land
For the first 4 billion years of the Earth's history the land was completely barren. With no roots to bind the particles of sand and mud together, there was no soil. Every breeze was laden with dust and rivers ran thick with mud. Of all the dusty colours of mud and rock, one was missing everywhere – green.

Insects from the sea
As plant life advanced over the Earth another group of living creatures, the insects, moved from the sea to take advantage of this enormous new supply of food. The insects were adaptations of ancient sea-living segmented worms. Perhaps the first to crawl out of the sea were primitive millipedes that grew to lengths of up to 2 m. Following the millipedes came the meat-eating centipedes, spiders and scorpions. The scorpions already had relatives living in the sea at this period, catching fish in their monstrous pincers. Dragonflies were among the most primitive animals to take to the air. Flying insects could glide from tree to tree without returning to the ground where hungry animals might be waiting. Other ancient winged insects included cockroaches, grasshoppers and locusts.

Soon plants developed roots and leaves. Roots enabled plants to support themselves and to reach water hidden deeper in the soil. Leaves helped the plant use the sunlight to build new plant material. A race for the skies had begun; the taller plant could take the sunlight from its neighbour, and so generation by generation it made more seedlings, growing higher and higher. Within a few million years there were forests, and soon the forests had spread to most of the wet areas of the Earth. These forests rose 30 m into the sky, and were built from three kinds of primitive plant: giant horsetails, club mosses and ferns.

How coal was made
The first swamp forests grew in the lowlands through which flowed meandering rivers that became silted up with mud as they neared the sea. Fallen logs piled up in the stagnant water, covered with mud and sand from the rivers. These layers of tree trunks were squeezed together, and the black mass of rotten wood eventually turned into a rock known as coal. So the age of the first forests is also the age when much coal was formed in Europe and North

America, which is why it is known as the 'Carboniferous', linked to the French word for coal, *charbon*. In coal you can still sometimes find remains of things that lived in the forest.

About 400 million years ago, fish took their first steps onto the land, probably to search for new supplies of food. At first the primitive fish jumped out of the water to catch a passing insect – just like the modern trout, but one group of fish eventually acquired the skills to pursue insects across the muddy swamps. These first land-walkers are known as 'amphibians', animals equally at home in the water and on the land.

For the first few tens of millions of years, the amphibians were rulers of the land and grew to the size of crocodiles. Around 250 million years ago, almost all of these early amphibians became extinct because they were unable to compete with the more adaptable reptiles and dinosaurs.

Life on land

FINS were useless out of water, so the air-breathing landfish rapidly evolved legs. The leg bones, wrist bones and finger bones of the landfish developed from the lobe-shaped fins of the bony fish. But life on land requires much more than legs!

A fish does not need to support its own weight because it is buoyed up by water. But these first amphibians had to grow strong backbones bound with muscles so that they could support themselves.

One of the strangest-looking early amphibians was *Diplocaulus* (below right, main illustration) with its flattened triangular-shaped head. Like aircraft wings, this shape gave the animal lift; it probably lay on the bottom of a river and rose rapidly to grab its prey.

DIPNORHYNCHUS

GRIPHOGNATHUS

CACOPS

DIADECTES

Air-breathing fish

The fish that first left the water were related to the coelacanths (see page 23). We can only guess at what change in the environment triggered an isolated group of fish to become air breathing. A small group of fish may have learned to live out of water by adapting to survive in the mud, formed when a lake or river dried out each year in the summer heat. Increased competition for food may have led some fish to search for prey around the water's edge and thereby gain advantage over other fish.

Whatever the specific circumstances, once the skill of air-breathing had been acquired a whole new environment was opened up, and small populations of air-breathing fish rapidly expanded to become the ancestors of all the subsequent land animals. Two of the earliest of these air-breathing fish were *Griphognathus* and *Dipnorhynchus*. These early creatures were 'almost amphibians' and are known to have lived in western Australia and Europe. They grew to a length of almost 1 m.

ICHTHYOSTEGA FOSSIL

Icthyostega
Skeletons of some of the earliest amphibians are found in rocks in Greenland, not then a frozen continent of mountains and ice, but a land of warm, rainy lowlands near to the equator. *Ichthyostega* still has a head and a tail like a fish, but its legs show that it was able to walk on dry land. However, it is unlikely that it would have strayed far from water. On land it moved awkwardly, swinging its body from side to side. With its sharp teeth it probably lived chiefly on fish, although it varied this diet with a selection of juicy worms and millipedes.

DID YOU KNOW?

***Vieraella*, the oldest-known frog, was tiny – only 3 cm long. *Paleobatrachus* is another primitive frog whose tadpoles have also been fossilised. Modern frogs have developed methods of protecting their tadpoles. The male of the Pipa toad sticks the eggs on the female's back where, covered with a thin skin, they turn into tadpoles under her protection. Another frog from southern Chile hatches its eggs inside the male frog's mouth, until, with a burp, out jump the tiny froglets.**

While all amphibians pass through a fish-like stage when they are newly hatched, some species grow into adult-sized fish-like babies. Some species of Mexican salamander stay in a fish stage, their gills protruding from their necks like small bushes. The Aztecs called them water servants or 'axolotls'.

The amphibians that survived gave up their lives as large, land-based monsters and became small, water-loving creatures.

Some of the most familiar modern amphibians, the frogs, evolved only around 200 million years ago. Their hunched bodies and strong rear legs were designed for jumping movements. Around the same time another group of modern amphibians appeared including newts, salamanders and the strange worm -like caecilians which have no legs and, like snakes, possess as many as 200 vertebrae in their spines.

An early reptile
One of the earliest-known reptiles was *Hylonomus*, which looked very like a modern-day lizard. It lived in dry vegetation where it hunted insects and worms. *Hylonomus* had sharp teeth which allowed it to eat even insects with tough skins, such as millipedes.

HYLONOMUS

Early amphibians lived near the water, where they laid their eggs and found their food. About 350 million years ago, forests spread over the land and this new supply of food encouraged one group of amphibians to abandon the water. They had found a new way to produce their children: in eggs provided with a yolk. The egg was one of the most successful designs in the long history of evolution.

The egg itself was not new. A number of amphibians and fish had even developed eggs sufficiently well-protected to survive in moist soil. However, this new egg contained a food supply in

Evolution of the egg

EVOLUTION is always working through innovations that allow animals to become more plentiful. The best way to increase the survival of a species is to protect newborn animals. Most primitive animals release millions of their young into the water and only a tiny proportion are likely to survive. The amphibians and fish laid lots of unprotected eggs in water, most of which end up as food for predators. The hard-shelled egg protected baby reptiles until they were big enough to survive in the outside world. By laying nutrient-rich and better defended eggs, reptiles did not need to produce as many eggs to make sure enough children survived. These eggs made reptiles very successful, allowing them to live almost anywhere.

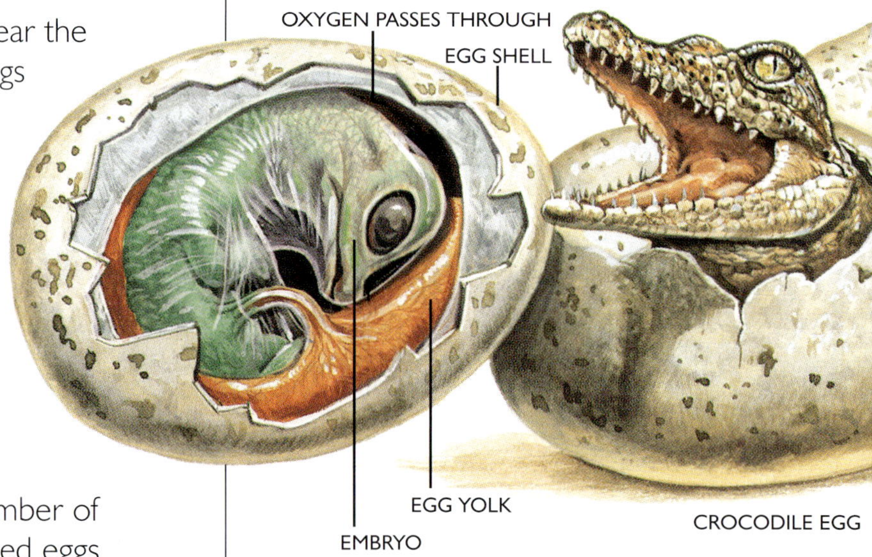

SCUTOSAURUS

Tortoises and turtles
Tortoises and turtles have lived on Earth for more than 200 million years. They are well adapted to their environments and, by retreating into their hard shell, they can defend themselves well against predators. Tortoises kept to the land and turtles lived in the sea. The turtle *Archelon* grew to a length of 3.5 m.

PROGANOCHELYS

ARCHELON

TESTUDO

A spiny sail

DIMETRODON had a giant spiny sail along its back. The sail worked as a kind of solar radiator. Reptiles are cold blooded and to be agile must be warmed in the sun. By angling its sail to catch the sun's rays, and by passing its blood through the membrane that ran between the spines, the creature could warm itself quickly at dawn, and so become the most active among the reptiles in the morning. Should it get overheated in the noonday sun, its sail could be angled into the wind, to radiate excess heat away, into the air.

DIMETRODON

Armoured plant-eaters

P*AREIASAURUS* and *Scutosaurus* were the largest of the early reptiles alive around 280 million years ago. They were about the size of rhinoceroses and had thick bony plates embedded in their skin. Both developed limbs beneath the body, so that they could walk in a more upright position. This characteristic was to be perfected by the dinosaurs (*see pages 32–33 and 38–39*). Throughout the history of land animals, the largest of all creatures alive at any time have been the herbivores, which were able to grow big as they fed on the abundant forest plant food. The armour plating on these giant reptiles shows that size alone was not enough to protect them from fiercer, but smaller, reptile carnivores. *Pareiasaurus* and *Scutosaurus* lived in eastern Europe, in a region rich in the vegetation they relied on for food.

the yolk for the developing embryo, and a shell that allowed gases, such as oxygen, to pass through it so that the developing animal did not suffocate. It also could be laid buried in dry sand and earth – out of sight of hungry amphibians and free from any accompanying odour to give its location away.

Over the generations, as the shell became thicker to offer greater protection, so the baby inside had to grow bigger and stronger to break its way free.

Marine reptiles

ANOTHER two groups of reptiles moved back to the water, using their speed and size to hunt and live off the rich supplies of fish. The plesiosaurs developed land-legs into large paddles and the necks became elongated like seals'. In the ichthyosaurs, the legs almost disappeared, creating a reptile that looked rather like a toothy dolphin.

PAREIASAURUS

PLESIOSAUR: MURAENOSAURUS

ICHTHYOSAUR: ICHTHYOSAURUS

PLESIOSAUR: LIOPLEURODON

The fact that the plesiosaurs looked like seals and the ichthyosaurs resembled dolphins is not accidental. Both seals and dolphins are animals that formerly lived on land and became adapted for the sea only when the ichthyosaurs and plesiosaurs became extinct, about 65 million years ago. The Loch Ness monster was once thought to be a plesiosaur survivor, until a thorough search suggested that it does not exist.

Legless lizards

MOST modern reptiles belong to the group of diapsids that first appeared more than 300 million years ago. From the diapsids evolved the ancestors of most modern reptiles, including snakes. The chief feature of lizards and snakes is the flexibility and power of their jaws. Snakes also discovered that the absence of legs could increase their speed in bushes and trees.

THE ERA OF GIANTS

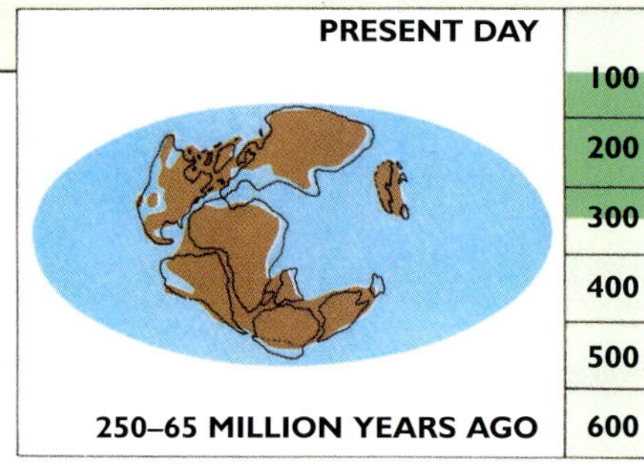

ABOUT 230 million years ago, one group of reptiles, known as the 'archosaurs', began to dominate all its rivals. From the archosaurs were to come the most spectacular land animals the world has ever known – the largest, the strongest and the fiercest. The archosaurs are more commonly known as the 'dinosaurs' from the Greek *deinos* meaning 'fearful' and *sauros*, 'lizard'. One branch of the archosaurs, the pterosaurs, took to the air and evolved into the largest creatures ever to fly in the Earth's skies. Another group of archosaurs slipped into the warm tropical rivers. Of all the unusual variety of archosaurs that ruled the land for more than 150 million years, only this last group, the crocodiles, survives today.

CHASMATOSAURUS

ERYTHROSUCHUS

Some of the earliest archosaurs resemble the original crocodiles. *Chasmatosaurus* caught fish with its sharp teeth. *Erythrosuchus* was the largest of the early dinosaurs, growing up to 5 m long.

The evolution of dinosaurs

The dinosaurs became larger, faster and more fierce as they competed with each other for food. For some plant-eating (herbivorous) dinosaurs, the only defence against the terrible meat-eating (carnivorous) dinosaurs was size. Complete skeletons of the gigantic *Brachiosaurus* are 23 m long and 12.6 m tall; some specimens may have grown up to 35 m.

An alternative defence was armour. *Stegosaurus* was 9 m long, with bony plates along its spine and a tail armed with a club of spines. Some carnivorous dinosaurs were fast moving. *Deinonychus* probably hunted in packs. *Megalosaurus* and *Allosaurus* both relied on their huge size and power to kill their prey.

The first crocodiles

The crocodiles and alligators of today have changed little from the time, 200 million years ago, when their ancestors lived in western America and swam in rivers and estuaries alongside the dinosaurs. They remain one of the largest and most remarkable of the 'living fossils'. However today's specimens would be dwarfed by the biggest of all known crocodiles: the fearsome *Deinosuchus*, that lived around 80 million years ago and grew to a length of 15 m.

1 COELOPHYSIS
2 TERATOSAURUS
3 ANCHISAURUS
4 RIOJASAURUS
5 STEGOSAURUS
6 DIPLODOCUS
7 BRACHIOSAURUS
8 MEGALOSAURUS
9 SAUROPELTA
10 ALLOSAURUS
11 DEINONYCHUS
12 IGUANODON

DEINOSUCHUS

REBUILDING DINOSAURS

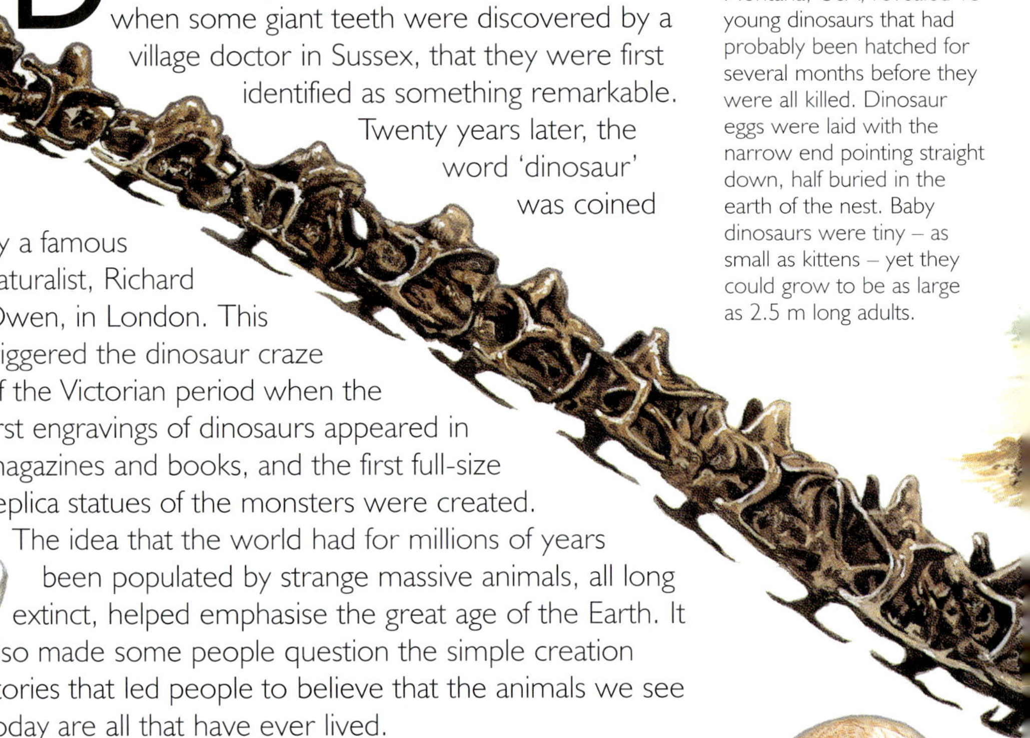

DINOSAUR bones have been dug up for hundreds of years, but it was not until 1820, when some giant teeth were discovered by a village doctor in Sussex, that they were first identified as something remarkable. Twenty years later, the word 'dinosaur' was coined by a famous naturalist, Richard Owen, in London. This triggered the dinosaur craze of the Victorian period when the first engravings of dinosaurs appeared in magazines and books, and the first full-size replica statues of the monsters were created.

The idea that the world had for millions of years been populated by strange massive animals, all long extinct, helped emphasise the great age of the Earth. It also made some people question the simple creation stories that led people to believe that the animals we see today are all that have ever lived.

Many of the best dinosaur finds have come from the dry western states of the United States. More than 100 years ago, dinosaur hunters explored the western states

Removing bones
When fossil dinosaur bones are discovered it is best to remove large masses of the rock surrounding them. The bones can also be covered by plaster for extra protection (1).

①

The blocks are then taken to a laboratory, where the bones can be carefully removed, perhaps with delicate dental drills and needles (2).

②

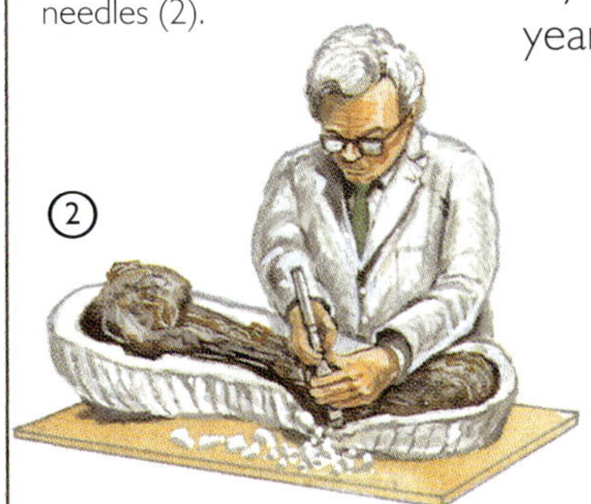

Large amounts of surrounding rock may also be removed by dissolving it in acid (3).

③

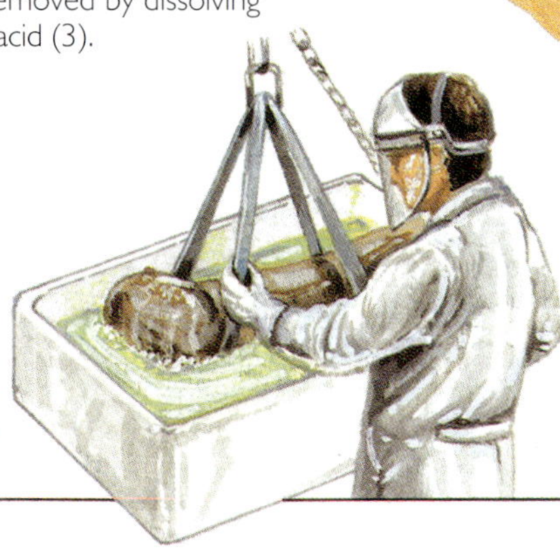

Dinosaur eggs
A fossil nest found in Montana, USA, revealed 15 young dinosaurs that had probably been hatched for several months before they were all killed. Dinosaur eggs were laid with the narrow end pointing straight down, half buried in the earth of the nest. Baby dinosaurs were tiny – as small as kittens – yet they could grow to be as large as 2.5 m long adults.

DINOSAUR EGG

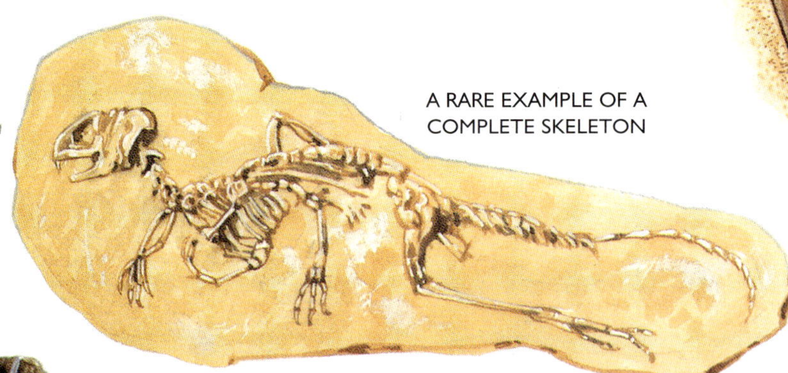

A RARE EXAMPLE OF A COMPLETE SKELETON

DINOSAUR BONES

Unlike seashells, it is extremely rare to find a dinosaur skeleton preserved exactly where the animal lived. After an animal has died the flesh will quickly be eaten, and the bones may be washed away. What at first sight appears to be a complete dinosaur skeleton all too often turns out to be a random collection of bones, washed together from many different skeletons.

of Colorado and Wyoming, transporting the bones back to the east coast by cart and train. In 30 years, around 130 new types of dinosaur were discovered.

One question that scientists have not been able to answer satisfactorily from fossil remains is whether dinosaurs were warm- or cold-blooded. Some features of the dinosaurs resemble the warm-blooded mammals and birds on Earth today, but this may be because the dinosaurs lived at a very warm period of the Earth's history. Many dinosaurs were extremely large, and it is known that the bigger the body of an animal, the longer it can retain its heat. It seems that dinosaurs could respond to temperature changes, like warm-blooded animals, but without needing to consume as much energy.

Dinosaur dispute
The leading 19th-century dinosaur hunters, O.C. Marsh and E.D. Cope, became sworn enemies when Marsh showed that Cope had assembled a dinosaur skeleton with the head on the wrong end!

MAIASAURA ('MOTHER LIZARD') NEST AND EGGS

RECONSTRUCTED SKELETON OF DIPLODOCUS

COELOPHYSIS FOOTPRINTS

Fossil footprints
Fossil footprints show how dinosaurs moved. Some walked on four legs, others on two; some lumbered slowly, while the small bird-like dinosaurs moved at great speed.

BRACHIOSAURUS FOOTPRINTS

Reconstructing the dinosaurs
Many of the early dinosaur finds were assembled incorrectly. If the exact structure of the skeleton can be assembled, the soft-bodied parts of the dinosaur can be reconstructed. This also helps us to understand the dinosaur's lifestyle. For example, the shape of the hips reveals how dinosaurs moved; while the pattern of the teeth tells us whether the animal tore at meat or chewed fibrous plants and trees.

Cycads and conifers
For more than 200 million years, the world's forests were built only from the evergreen trees, in particular the conifers and cycads. Both produced cones which had to be fertilised by pollen blown by the wind, a very inefficient means of reproduction which needed the release of large quantities of pollen to make sure that some might land on another cone. While conifers and some cycads are still found today, they no longer dominate the tropical forests.

FOSSIL OF A CONIFER CONE

The first flowers

MAGNOLIA FLOWER

Sometimes two separate groups of living things have evolved together, changing in tune with one another. Perhaps the most remarkable example is that of the flowers and the insects. Their dependence on each other has become very strong: the insect distributes the pollen made by the flowers, allowing flowers to become the seeds from which new plants grow. In exchange, the plant feeds the insect.

The attraction of flowers

FLOWERS have to use colour, scent and design to entice insects to visit them. Flowers have competed with one another over millions of years to attract the greatest number of insect visitors to ensure pollination. Most flowers are more brightly coloured towards their centres because that is where the pollen is found that brushes against the insect's body as it sucks at the flower's sweet nectar. Some flowers use colours at the infra-red end of the visible light spectrum. These colours are invisible to humans. Flowers also developed

GINGKO LEAVES

GINGKO FOSSIL

The gingko
Deciduous trees, many of which lose their leaves in winter, were the largest of the new flowering plants. Their flowers were often not as obvious or as colourful as their smaller relations. The maidenhair or gingko tree is a 'living fossil' from around 100 million years ago, when such trees were extremely common. The tree was found to survive in a small mountainous area in China. Seedlings from these survivors have now been planted in many gardens around the world. Fossil gingko leaves are found in the same rocks as dinosaur bones.

ABOUT 100 million years ago, a group of plants developed special coloured leaves and improved the taste of their pollen so that insects would come to call. These were the first flowers, like the magnolia and the water lily. The beetles became peppered with pollen, which was brushed against the next flower that they visited.

FOSSIL FLOWER

The southern beech
One of the oldest flowering trees is the *Nothofagus* or southern beech. *Nothofagus* forests are today scattered around the world – in South America, New Zealand, Australia and New Guinea. More than 150 million years ago, all these continents were part of the super-continent Gondwana, that was split into the present-day southern continents by the formation of new oceans. Leaf fossils show that 100 million years ago, *Nothofagus* forests also covered parts of Antarctica.

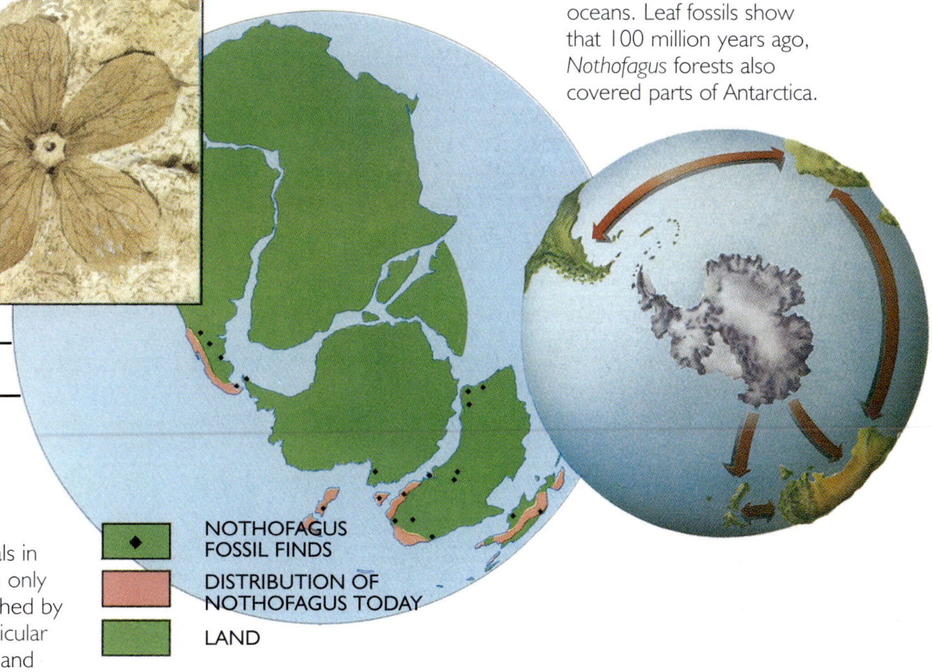

smells to attract insects. Some flowers produce the stench of rotten meat, particularly enticing to flies.

In order to increase the chance of reproduction, the challenge for all flowers is to attract insects that have recently visited another flower of the same species. In order to get such visits, some flowers evolved complex trumpet-shaped petals in which the nectar can only be reached by a particular size and shape of insect.

Insects have developed all kinds of different forms of communication. Many use sounds; grasshoppers rub their jagged legs against their wings, while cicadas click their abdomens like metal cans. Other insects use their highly sensitive sense of smell to pick up the individual complex scent of a male or female. They can recognise these scents at great distances, even when only the tiniest particle is carried in the air.

The most unusual flowers of all have given up attracting insects with rewards of delicious food. Instead, like the Late Spider orchid, they have grown to resemble the female of one type of bumblebee with such precision that the male arrives to mate with the flower. The sundew plant lures the insect not to carry the pollen as the orchid does but to catch and eat the insect.

Even after the land had been conquered, there remained another realm waiting to be populated: that of the air. There were two groups of descendants of the ancient reptiles, known as the archosaurs. First there were the strange, sinister pterosaurs; later, another group of animals that seem less strange to us because they are so familiar – the birds.

To be a successful flier a light but powerful body is required. Both the pterosaurs and the birds gradually lost much of the excess weight that they had inherited from their reptile ancestors. Their bones became thinner and hollow, and some species replaced their teeth with beaks. They also had to develop more powerful and active muscles, in order to be able to move their wings.

The flying reptiles

THE pterosaurs were all sizes, from the pigeon-sized *Eudimorphodon*, to *Quetzalcoatlus* with a wingspan of over 15 metres. By around 100 million years ago, the pterosaurs were well developed: *Pteranodon*, for example, had a head shaped like a rudder, and a beak big enough to carry fish.

While the pterosaurs ruled the air for about 100 million years, they eventually became extinct. They lost control of the air to another group of flying reptiles, the birds, who had found a more resilient material than stretched skin for wings: feathers.

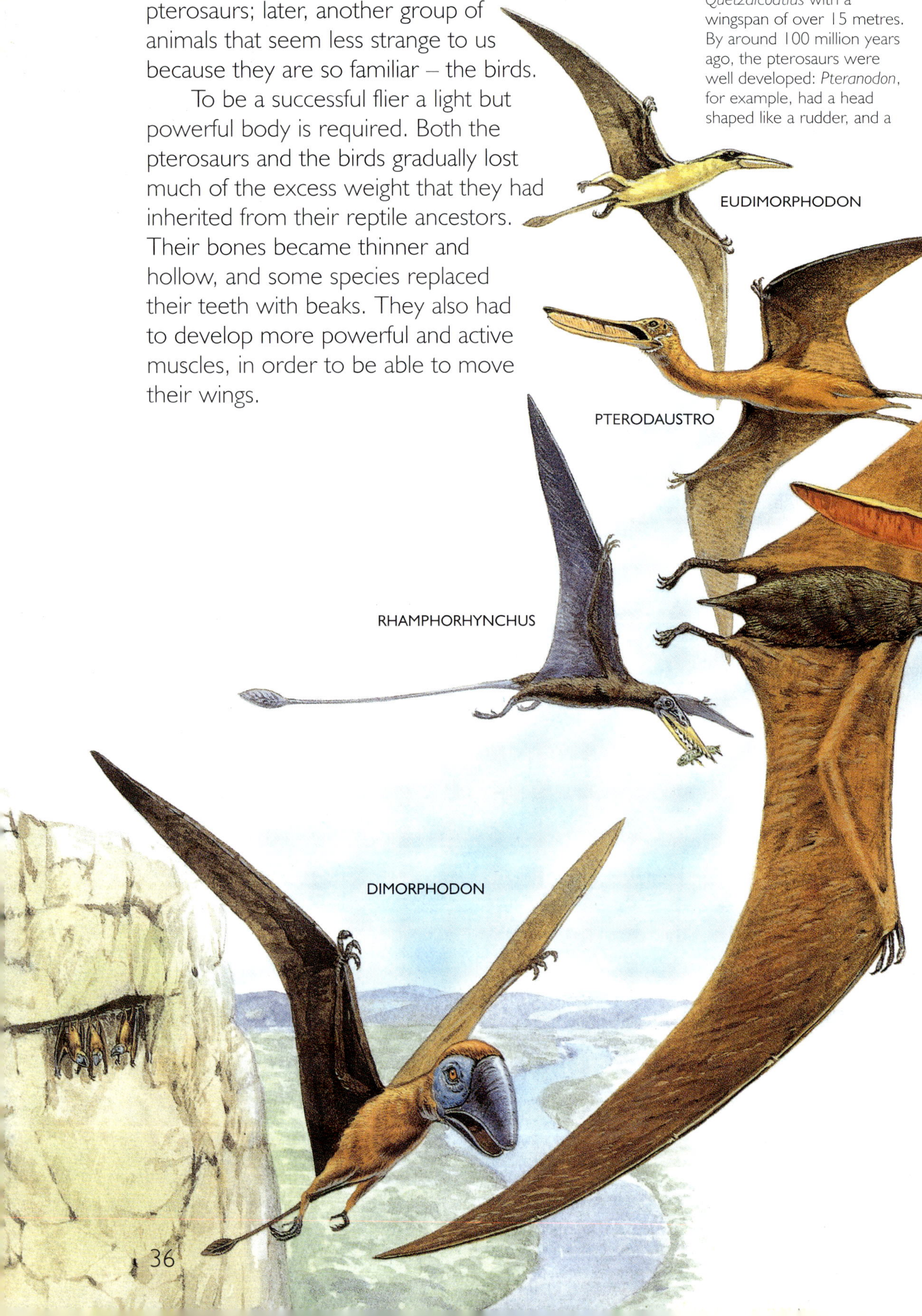

The missing link

DID YOU KNOW?

The wing of a pterosaur was extremely vulnerable. This was because it was made of stretched skin which, if it were torn or scratched, could not heal. The feathers of a bird's wing are ideal for flight: they are light and easily replaced if damaged. They also provide warmth for a chick, colour in the peacock's tail, and allow the hummingbird to hover in the cup of an orchid.

PTEROSAUR WING

BIRD WING

Feathers evolved first as an insulator, helping regulate the temperature of the original reptile ancestor of the birds.

A variety of birds

Seventy million years ago, loons, grebes, cormorants, primitive pelicans, ibises, rails and sandpipers were already common. These birds, whose descendants are alive today, lived alongside the dinosaurs for the last few million years of their reign. Other birds alive today have ancient ancestors too: *Presbyornis* was an early equivalent of the duck; *Argentavis* was one of the original vultures.

PRESBYORNIS

ARGENTAVIS

Ancient modern birds

Archaeopteryx may not have been a direct ancestor of modern birds, but only ten million years later we find fossils of birds similar to those alive today.

Hesperornis, shown here catching fish, was a flightless diving bird and probably an ancestor of the modern-day grebe. It was able to dive 2 m below the surface of the water.

SOME of the first known primitive birds date from around 150 million years ago – the time of the rise of the dinosaurs. The first, called *Archaeopteryx*, was found as a fossil in a German quarry. For a long time, many people considered it a fake, but now that other specimens of half-bird, half-reptile fossils have been found, *Archaeopteryx* is recognised to be one of a range of 'missing links' between the reptiles and the birds. Other fossils of similar age reveal the existence of a range of feathered reptiles and primitive birds. These provide an almost complete chain of missing-link animals that led to the development of the birds. *Archaeopteryx* was probably a poor flier. It had small claws on the front of its wings for clinging to branches.

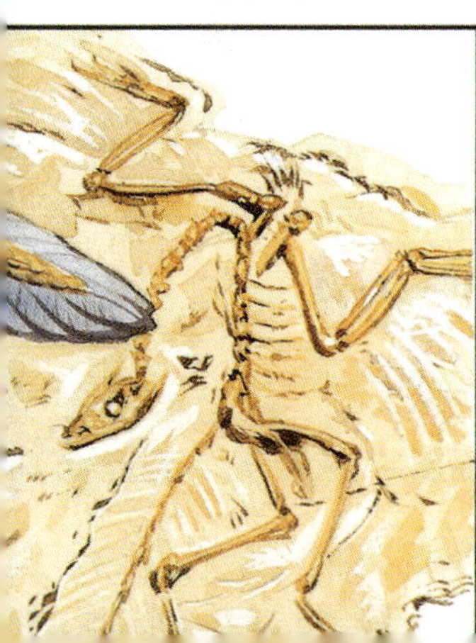

Birds that do not fly

BIRDS living on islands free from predators often grew large. When these birds' ancestors first flew to the remote ocean islands, they discovered that they were free of bigger competitors. Over millions of years they lost the ability to fly and grew to take the place of the large land animals. *Di*, or the moa, of New Zealand was taller than the 3-m-tall elephant bird of Madagascar. Used to living without fear, both were defenceless when humans arrived, with their dogs and rats. Both birds are now extinct.

AEPYORNIS (ELEPHANT BIRD)

DINORNIS (MOA)

Intelligent dinosaurs
One group among the latest dinosaurs, the bird-like ornithomimosaurs, was also probably the most intelligent. Their front legs were grasping claws, and they had large eyes and big brains. Like ostriches, these dinosaurs had powerful running legs and a counterbalancing tail. They would have moved very quickly, pouncing on their prey and escaping at speed. Instead of teeth, they had horny, bird-like beaks.

The tiny head of the *Saurornithoides* housed a large brain too. Its large eyes suggest it may have hunted at night, looking for small mammals and reptiles to eat.

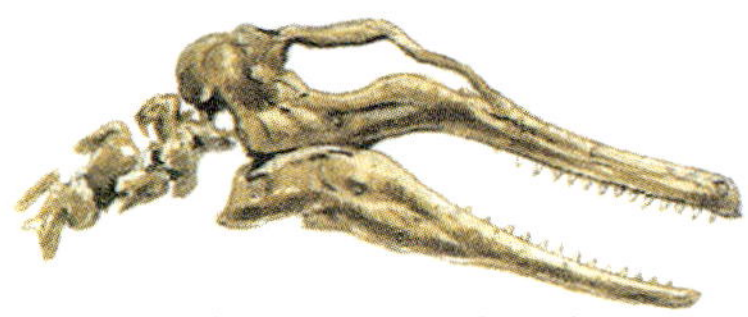
SKULL OF SAURORNITHOIDES

The last dinosaurs

HADROSAURS, or duckbilled dinosaurs, were some of the most common dinosaurs to have lived in the last few million years of the dinosaurs' reign. Their distinguishing feature was a large solid bone hump on their noses. Their mouths were designed for chewing the fibrous new flowering plants and trees that had taken over the world's forests a few million years earlier. Of all the duckbilled dinosaurs, *Parasaurolophus* was one of the most unusual. It had a hollow bone crest on its skull up to 1.8 m long. Hadrosaurs provided walking larders for the fiercesome *Tyrannosaurus* that

The reign of the 'terrible lizards', the dinosaurs, lasted for almost 150 million years. Throughout this period the dinosaurs were by far the largest, fiercest and strongest of all the land animals.
Some of the later dinosaurs were the most remarkable. The *Ankylosaur* had sides lined with spikes, its body protected with thick plates of bony armour. At the end of its tail was a heavy club of bone.

Since the early days of the dinosaurs, the climate of North America had changed and most of the region had become thickly forested. These swampy jungles were home to the duckbilled dinosaurs such as the hadrosaurs. However, such conditions were far from ideal for one of the last of the long-necked dinosaurs, the 21 m *Alamosaurus (see right)*, that lived in the drier, open plains.

Many tiny land mammals survived the catastrophe that killed off the last dinosaurs. They lived by scavenging small animals and insects, and could easily find shelter by burrowing in the ground, or hiding in holes in rocks.

ZALAMBDALESTES

had a massive head mounted on a powerful muscular neck; its jaw armed with a set of 15-cm-long curved-dagger teeth.

One of the few dinosaurs that even *Tyrannosaurus* would have avoided attacking was the plant-eating dinosaur *Triceratops* that charged at its enemies with its massive head, wreathed with an edging of solid bone and crowned with three massive forward-pointing horns.

End of the dinosaurs

The dinosaurs were large animals, and so they were vulnerable to any temporary loss of their food supply. The massive plant-eating dinosaurs would have been the first to starve if the forests had died back. Without the source of plant-eating dinosaur flesh, the meat-eaters would soon have died too. Dinosaurs were also poorly adapted to the cold.

The catastrophe that led to the death of the forests may have been caused by something from outside the Earth. It is likely that an asteroid – a 20-km mass of rock speeding through space – collided with the Earth. Such a collision may have led to worldwide fires, and a month or more of darkness when the atmosphere was so filled with dust and smoke that the sun's light and warmth could not get through. Even the tropical forests would have been plunged into darkness and a deep frost would have followed, killing much of the plant life.

We can tell something of what happened at this time by looking at the animals that survived. These were the tiny land animals and the dinosaurs' relatives, the crocodiles. The pterosaurs died out but birds, with their warm layer of feathers, survived.

SITES WHERE ASTEROIDS HAVE HIT THE EARTH

Evidence in the rocks

IN ROCKS that were formed on the seafloor at the time the dinosaurs disappeared, there are particles of charcoal from massive continent-wide forest fires. There are also fragments of damaged rock from some massive explosion. Around the Caribbean Sea, colossal waves, hundreds of metres high, burst over the land carrying enormous boulders, suggesting that the asteroid may have crashed somewhere nearby. The remains of a giant crater may lie along the coast of Yucatán, Mexico.

THE EARLY MAMMALS

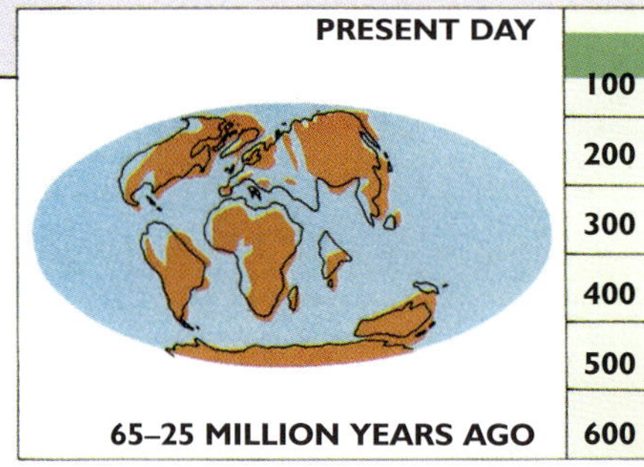

SIXTY-FIVE million years ago, the thundering of the great dinosaurs had all gone; in their place tiny mammals, not much larger than mice, began to occupy an empty world. For 150 million years, while the dinosaurs ruled the land, they had survived only by staying small, hiding, and hunting chiefly at night. As the trees and plants grew back after the devastation that had killed the dinosaurs, so these tiny mammals gradually became larger, developing into the ancestors of many of the most familiar living animals; from whales to lions, from cows to humans.

The mammals gave birth to live young who were then fed with their mother's milk. This was an innovation in evolution as important as the reptile's egg. It ensured that the babies survived the dangerous journey of early life through into adulthood. Unlike the reptiles, mammals had also learned to keep their bodies at a constant temperature, whatever the outside temperature. Mammals also evolved hair from the reptile's scales, just as the birds had evolved feathers, to keep themselves warm.

The first mammals
The original mammals were large and evolved from the reptiles around 250 million years ago. By 200 million years ago, there were mammals the size of a shrew, with a relatively large brain, that hunted insects at night.

Among the mammals that lived around the time of the death of the dinosaurs was *Zalambdalestes* which looked like a shrew with a long snout. Its powerful legs were actually elongated feet. It grew to around 20 cm in length, and probably lived in the undergrowth, running and jumping in its search for insects, which it would catch with its long sharp teeth.

The spread of the mammals

After the dinosaurs had gone, mammals increased in size. *Ptilodus* was like a modern squirrel; *Miacis* looked like a modern pine marten, while *Purgatorius* was probably an ancestor of the monkeys. A separate group of marsupial mammals first appeared in South America. Around 100 million years ago, the Gondwana supercontinent broke up, leaving Australian marsupials completely isolated from all the other later varieties of mammals *(see map)*.

Living reptile-mammals

TWO of the halfway reptile-mammals are still alive today, in Australia. The duckbilled platypus and the spiny anteater are both hairy, like a mammal, but lay eggs like a reptile. When they are hatched, the newborn babies feed on milk from the sweat glands on their mother's belly: these are the origin of nipples.

THE SPREAD OF MARSUPIALS ABOUT 65 MILLION YEARS AGO

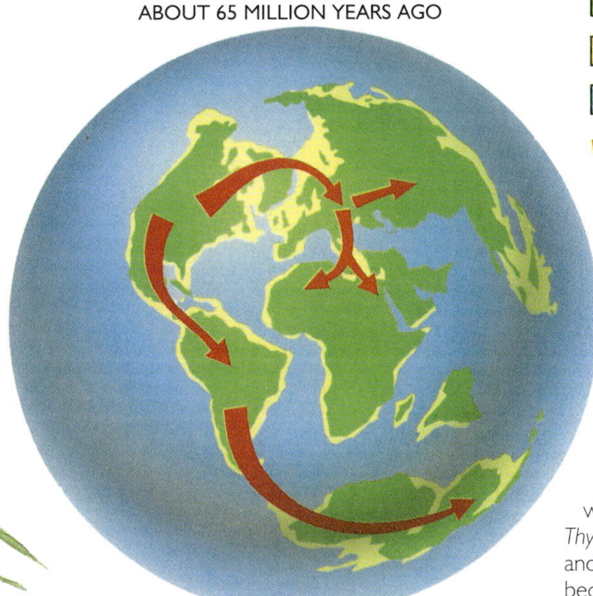

PRESENT-DAY CONTINENTS

CONTINENTAL SHELF

SEA

MOVEMENT OF MARSUPIALS

Australian marsupials

On their island continent, Australian marsupials evolved into almost exactly the same range of large (placental) mammals (see pages 44-45) found in the other continents. There were marsupial 'cats' like *Thylacoleo*, marsupial 'moles' and, until 1933 when they became extinct, a marsupial 'wolf' that was last recorded in captivity on the island of Tasmania. More than 40,000 years ago, before the arrival of the first men to Australia, there lived a giant marsupial the size and shape of a rhino, called *Diprotodon*. Also a victim of hunting and environmental change was the largest-ever kangaroo, *Procoptodon*.

PREHISTORIC CLIMATE

Moving southwards
Fifty million years ago, Antarctica was warm and thickly forested. However, as the continent drifted to the south the trees all died. About 15 million years ago, the land became covered in ice. This frozen continent has chilled the whole Earth and, in the past million years, brought a series of ice ages.

THE OVERALL pattern of different climates between the equator and the poles has always existed. However, during most of the past 600 million years there were no ice caps, and the whole Earth was much warmer. During this time, warm, subtropical conditions extended into regions of northern Europe and northern America. During the past 50 million years the world has been generally cooling. The range of plants growing in North America suggests that there was a sharp decrease in average temperatures about 40 million years ago.

Averaged out over many years, the measurements of temperature and rainfall that we call weather will indicate the climate of a region. Climate, however, includes not just average conditions but the range of conditions that exists within that average. For example, months of persistent

ANTARCTICA: 50 MILLION YEARS AGO

Pangaea: the supercontinent
Between 400 and 250 million years ago, almost all the continents formed a single group: Pangaea. The centre of this huge landmass lay close to the equator where temperatures were probably hotter than any known on Earth today, so hot that few plants or animals could survive.

In deserts today, plants and animals store water in order to survive. Cacti

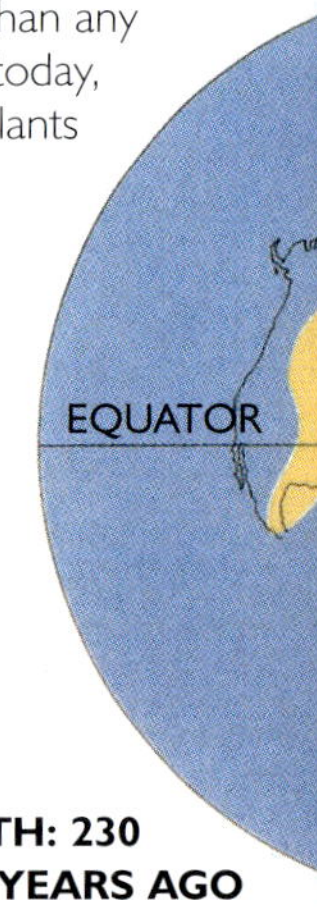

THE EARTH: 230 MILLION YEARS AGO

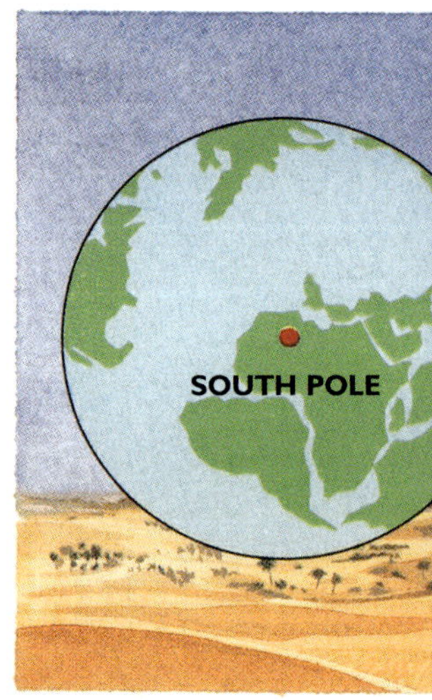

Hot and cold winds
The Earth is covered with a thin skin of atmosphere, less than 100 km thick, that is always in motion. Near the equator the sun is high in the sky, heating both the ground and the air. Close to the Earth's poles, the sun is never very high or strong, and in the middle of winter the sun does not rise for several months. These differences in temperature drive the Earth's winds. Hot air from the equator is light, and rises and spreads both northwards and southwards. Cold, heavy air from the poles moves towards the equator, close to the ground. The hot and cold air meet midway between the equator and the poles, creating the most changeable and complex weather in these middle latitudes. Large cyclonic storms form almost daily along the boundary between the warm and cold air-masses, rotating anti-clockwise in the northern hemisphere, and clockwise to the south of the equator.

use deep roots to tap water below the surface.

Closer to the coasts of Pangaea there were rainforests. Today, the tropical rainforest is the richest of all environments, in both number and variety of plants and animals. Many plants actually root in the upper canopy of the trees, where monkeys and parrots make their homes. Other animals prefer to live on the forest floor.

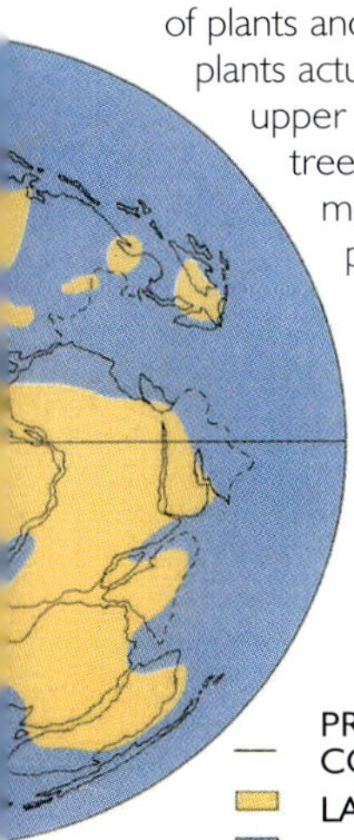

Ice ages
The oldest ice age yet discovered occurred about 2.3 billion years ago. There was an ice cap in the Sahara Desert 450 million years ago, when Africa was located close to the South Pole.

PATTERN OF WINDS

high or low temperatures, or months of high rainfall or no rainfall, also contribute to climate.

Plants are extremely sensitive to climate; some plants like the weather cool, others like it hot. Some plants need a continual supply of rain, while others store water in bulbs and can survive on a single thunder-shower once a year. The climate that plants 'measure' is particularly sensitive to the variability in temperatures or rainfall. Plants are particularly sensitive to extremes and it may only take one hard frost or one long drought to kill them.

Animals are just as dependent on the climate as plants. If the plants die, then so will the animals that eat them, as well as animals that eat other animals. If the rivers dry up in a drought, or become completely ice-bound in an intense freeze, then which animals survive will also be affected.

Moving northwards
Until around 100 million years ago, Europe and North America were joined, and therefore the climate history recorded in the rocks of the two regions is very similar. The joined continents spent the past 400 million years moving north, passing through the various climate zones that form bands parallel with the equator. Both regions lay in the desert belt, south of the equator, 400 million years ago, before moving into the equatorial zone around 350 million years ago, when they were covered in tropical rainforests. Over millions of years the remains of all the timber that fell into sinking swamps in these rainforests created thick seams of coal.

NORTH AMERICA: 350 MILLION YEARS AGO

NORTH AMERICA: TODAY

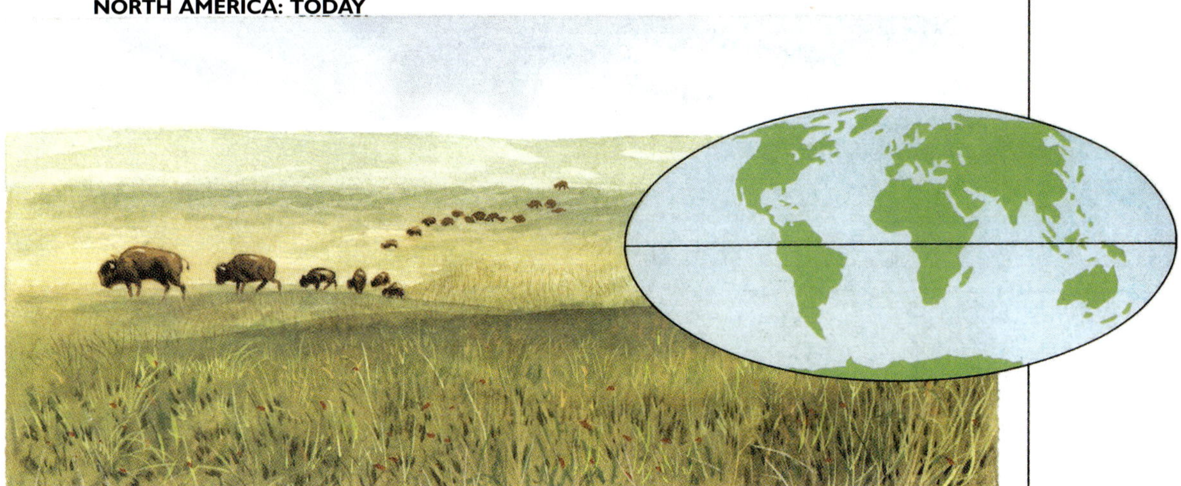

The edentates

In South America, a strange group of placental mammals evolved known as edentates, meaning 'animals with few or no teeth'. This group included the anteaters, the armadillos and the sloths.

Armadillos have been around for 60 million years. Some armadillo-like Glyptodonts grew very large. One of the largest grew to the size of a car – more than 3 m long and 1.5 m tall.

The ground sloths were the ancestors of the modern tree sloths, but grew up to 4 m long. These giant sloths died out only 11,000 years ago.

Anteaters had powerful claws, a long snout, and an even longer tongue. The modern equivalents of these anteaters are today found only in South America.

SLOTH: GLOSSOTHERIUM

ANTEATER: EUROTAMANDUA

ARMADILLO: GLYPTODON

The most important advance in mammal development came with the emergence of placental mammals. Placental mammals proved more successful than the marsupials, and whenever the two types came into direct competition (in Asia, Europe, North America and Africa) the marsupials all died out. South America is the only region in which the marsupials survived even after the placentals had arrived, but for long periods South America remained as an island isolated from the other continents. Australia was the only continent to separate from its neighbours before placental

AMPHICYON SUCKLING HER YOUNG

In placental mammals, babies remain much longer inside their mothers than in the marsupials. While in the womb, the baby is fed by the placenta, an organ that provides food and oxygen. These babies are exposed to fewer risks when they are tiny, and their chance of survival is increased.

The variety of mammals

AFTER they emerged to become the dominant form of land animal, mammals evolved into a wide variety of types and sizes. Yet all the different groups had ancestors that at the time of the dinosaurs were little larger than squirrels. *Hesperocyon*, a meat-eating ancestor of the modern jackals, wolves and dogs, was alive about 30 million years ago. At the same time *Nimravus*, a leopard-like cat, hunted in the forests of North America and Europe. *Diacodexis*, not much larger than a rabbit, was the ancestor of modern pigs and hippopotamuses,

EMBLOTHERIUM

INDRICOTHERIUM

DIACODEXIS

and lived 50 million years ago. The hoofed *Eobasileus*, alive around 40 million years ago, had six bony horns. The largest of all land mammals lived at this time in Asia: *Indricotherium*, a relation of the primitive rhinoceros family. It weighed up to 30 metric tons. At the same time lived the largest-known land mammal meat-eater, the vicious *Andrewsarchus*.

mammals had emerged. Placentals only arrived in Australia when accompanying human beings, a few tens of thousands of years ago.

By around 50 million years ago, large placental mammals had appeared in North America, Europe and Asia. Many of these already looked like the modern mammals into which they eventually evolved. Elephants developed trunks because their massive heads had to be supported on a thick, short neck that could not bend to reach the ground. The swamp-loving *Moeritherium* that flourished in Africa between 40 and 25 million years ago was related to the ancestors of the elephants, but weighed only as much as a pig. Horses first appeared around 50 million years ago, but when fully grown were no bigger than baby lambs.

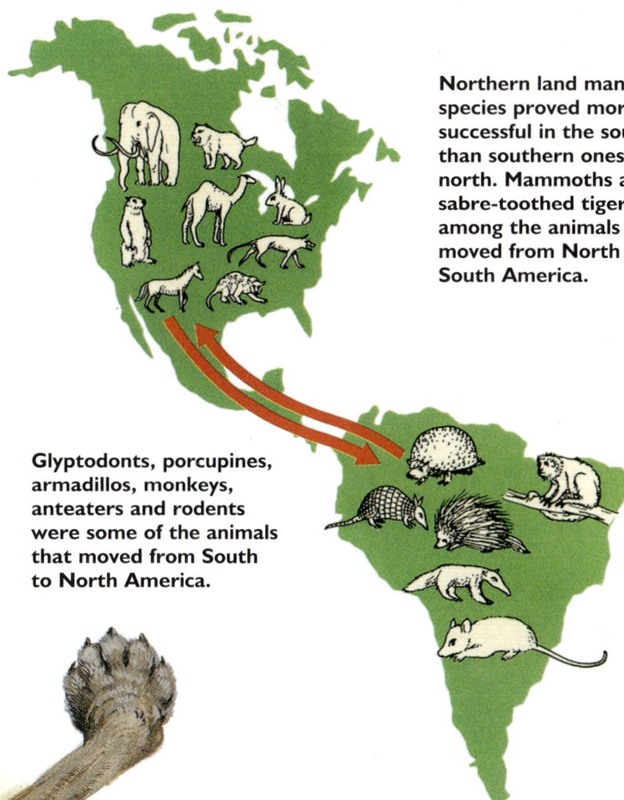

Mammal movements
Three million years ago, a permanent 'bridge' of land developed for the first time through Panama, linking South America with North America. Along this narrow corridor, covered with thick tropical vegetation, over the generations groups of animals from the north moved to the south, while some South American animals journeyed north. The placental invaders from the north proved to be better adapted than the marsupials and today, half the varieties of mammals in South America originally came from the north. However, only a few of the South American marsupial species, such as the armadillo, managed to survive in North America.

The bats were the third group of vertebrates (animals with backbones) to fly, following the pterosaurs, by now extinct, and the birds. The birds were highly successful and there was little possibility of the placental mammals competing with them. The solution was to occupy the part of the sky that most birds had not attempted to live in: the sky at night.

Other mammals came to live by the seashore. Over many generations, some of these mammals became better swimmers. They found an almost endless supply of fish in the sea.

The first bats

THE tiny, insect-eating mammals that lived alongside the dinosaurs had evolved a keen intelligence, and abilities to hunt and move at night. Some developed wings from the flaps of skin between the animal's fingers, which over many generations became more and more extended. Bats like *Icaronycteris* are known to have existed around 50 million years ago, and are little different to those alive today.

The first whales

The first fossil whales date from around 50 million years ago. They show us that the first whales were no larger than seals. *Pakicetus* was a meat-eater with sharp teeth. It spent part of its life ashore. Within a few million years, the hind legs of whales like *Protocetus* had become smaller, while the forelimbs changed into flippers and their bodies were more streamlined. Buoyed up by the water, and with ample food, the whales grew enormous. *Basilosaurus*, alive around 40 million years ago, was 20 m long.

As they moved to live in the water, the whales separated into two groups. The first group kept their teeth, and in time were to become the dolphins, porpoises and sperm whales. All were fish-eaters, intelligent and experts at tracking and catching their prey. *Eurhinodelphis* was another in this group. It had an elongated snout and lived around ten million years ago. In the second group, all the teeth were replaced by a mesh of baleen, made from hornlike material, with which whales sifted the water for tiny animals.

Gliding mammals

Gliding mammals first learned to fly by gliding from tree to tree on flaps of skin between their legs and body. Gliding is a useful means of tree-hopping, and also avoids enemies on the ground. Gliding mammals, such as *Planetetherium*, are thought to have lived around 50 million years ago.

DID YOU KNOW?

The closest living relative of the elephant is the dugong, or 'sea cow', that took to the sea about 50 million years ago. *Hydrodamalis*, an ancestor of the dugong evolved about 200,000 years ago.

***Paleoparadoxia* is a hippo-like creature that lived along the shores of western North America.**

Baleen whales

Cetotherium was a baleen whale alive around ten million years ago. Although *Cetotherium* was only 4 m long, the biggest of all animals today, the blue whale, is also a baleen whale. It feeds on the vast harvest of shrimp-like krill found in the southern oceans.

More marine mammals

Seals are related to dogs and cats, and are probably descended from an otter-like animal from about 30 million years ago. *Enialarctos* was alive 20 million years ago. Its land legs still resembled those of an otter, but its head already looked like a sea lion's. *Imagotaria* was a type of walrus that lived along the Pacific coast of North America between ten and five million years ago.

THE AGE OF THE HUMANS

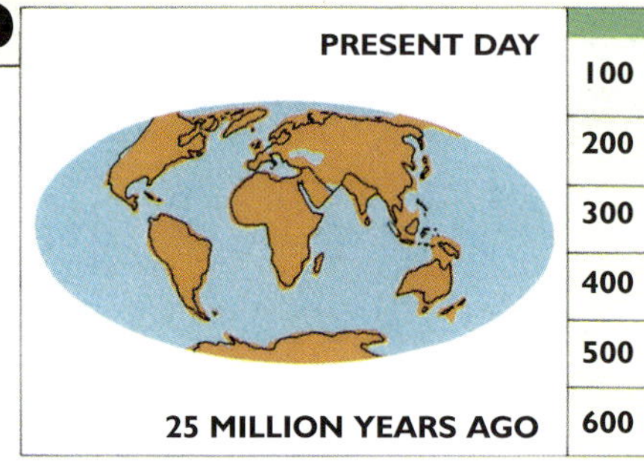

TODAY, THERE are around 200 different types of primate. Most live in trees. They have evolved flexible shoulder joints to allow them to swing from branches, as well as grasping hands and feet. Primates have closely spaced eyes on the front of a flat face. Using its large brain, a primate can construct rapid three-dimensional images of the world around it.

Primate babies gestate longer in their mother's womb, and they usually only arrive one at a time. Primate children are carefully tended and taught about the world by their parents. The rules by which primates organise their societies are often complicated, and to cope with the period of education necessary before adulthood, primates' lives are relatively long.

The earliest ancestors of the primates had already separated from the other small mammals by the end of the reign of the dinosaurs. One primate ancestor alive around 50 million years ago, the squirrel-like *Plesiadapis* *(see page 41)*, was common in western Europe and North America.

Primitive primates
Some primitive primates, alive around 40 million years ago, survive on the island of Madagascar off the east coast of Africa. Lemurs are small, night-dwelling animals. In Africa they failed to survive the competition from the larger apes and monkeys that came after them *(see pages 52-53)*. Like the lemurs alive today, *Necrolemur* and *Notharctus* had hands and feet that could grip branches. They were tree-dwellers and excellent tree-climbers.

Upright apes
By around two million years ago, two or three separate species of upright apes were probably living in East Africa. Only *Homo erectus* survived to become the ancestor of all humans.

EARLY HUMANS FIGHT OVER PRECIOUS FOOD

The monkeys

Monkeys evolved in two groups: New World monkeys mainly in South America, and Old World monkeys in Africa, Asia and Europe. New World monkeys have long tails. The apes evolved from the Old World monkeys in Africa.

NEW WORLD MONKEYS

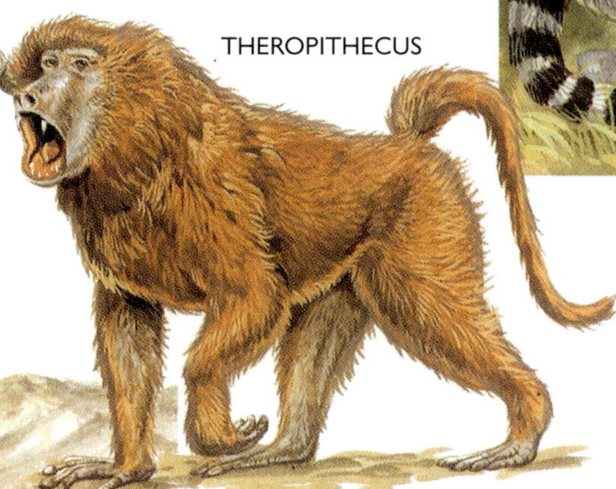

OLD WORLD MONKEYS

In Africa, seven million years ago, there was a separation in the line of evolution between the gorillas, the chimpanzees and an animal with a new skill: ape-humans who could walk upright.

Gigantic apes

Between twenty and ten million years ago, apes became very common in Africa. The climate was changing – the thick jungle making way for drier savannah grassland. In order to survive in this new environment it was necessary to learn to live down on the ground instead of high up in jungle treetops.

Around ten million years ago, some of these ground-apes moved into southern Asia. In China, *Gigantopithecus*, alive a million years ago, grew up to 2.5 m tall and weighed 270 kg.

Elephants and mammoths
The most spectacular of the northern Ice Age mammals were relatives of the elephant. *Platybelodon* lived eight million years ago and had strange, shovel-shaped tusks. *Anancus* had tusks between 3 and 4 m long. As the climate cooled, these animals grew thicker coats of hair, evolving into the mammoths, such as *Mammuthus columbi*.

About 15 million years ago the world became cooler, and a permanent cover of ice and snow formed across Antarctica. This was the start of the ice age. For the past two million years, in almost every part of the world, the environment has changed every hundred thousand years from cold to warm, and from wet to dry. In the cold periods, ice sheets spread to cover much of northern Europe, Canada and the north-eastern United States. At the edges of the ice sheets lay tundra, with its frozen soil. As the ice expanded south, so the climate zones that lay between the polar areas and the equator were squeezed, with areas that are now desert being forested areas with plentiful rain-fall, and parts of today's rainforests being arid grasslands. In between these glacial periods, the climate has been even warmer than it is today – so warm that hippopotamuses once lived in swamps in northern England. The last glacial period ended 10,000 years ago, but the climate has continued to change. As climates change, animal and plant species are forced to adapt to the new conditions in order to survive.

Ice age mammals

AROUND 30,000 years ago, at the height of the last glacial period, many large animals roamed Europe. To help keep them warm through the long cold winters, mammoths had thick woolly coats of hair, and stored fat obtained from feasts of summer plants. They may have used their long curved tusks to scrape away snow to uncover any

Changing sea levels

AS SNOW fell on the continents, the ice sheets built up to a thickness of 4 km, taking up water from the oceans until sea levels had fallen by 130 m. Islands became joined to the mainland, and a 'land-bridge' formed from Siberia to Alaska across the Bering Strait. Among the animals that travelled across this land-bridge out of North America were the horse, camel and lynx. Into North America moved the mammoth, bison, mountain sheep and goat, and musk-ox. Around 20,000 years ago, humans from Siberia walked across the tundra into America.

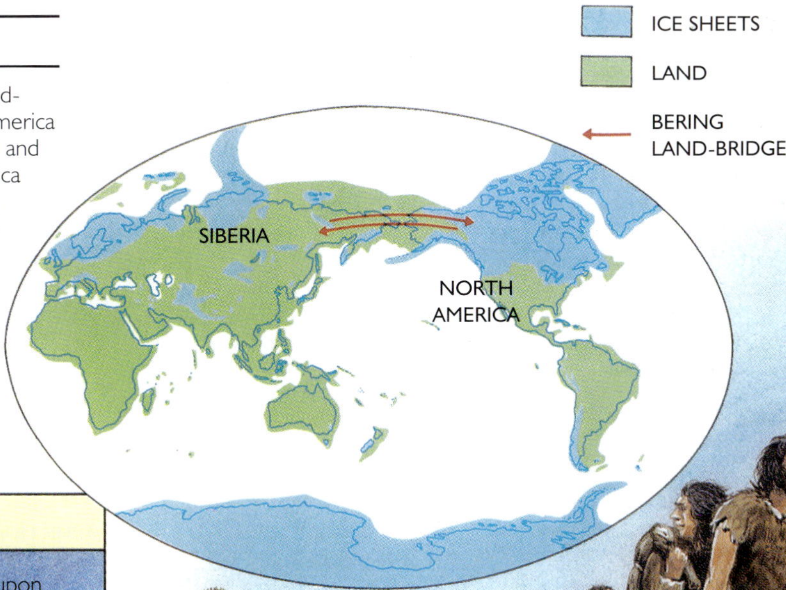

edible vegetation below.

Woolly rhinoceroses and grizzly bears lived alongside the mammoths. Lions and sabre-toothed tigers had an extra covering of fur, but they did not need to store fat as they could prey upon the other animals in both the winter and the summer. *Megaloceras*, also known as the Irish elk, was the largest of the deer, growing 2.5 m long.

Some of the most remarkable reconstructions of life in the ice age come from cave paintings in south-western France and northern Spain. They were drawn by people who lived 30,000 to 10,000 years ago. They show animals which lived at that time.

It is likely that hunting by humans helped to drive a number of animals, such as *Megatherium* from South America, to extinction. Animals' fear of humans today may have been acquired over the past few thousand years.

ISLAND LIFE

The trees of St Helena
The seeds of most trees are too heavy to be carried far by the wind, and too fragile to survive a long journey in water. On the island of St Helena in the Atlantic Ocean, relatives of the small sunflower and lettuce plants have evolved into five different types of tree, each between 4 and 6 m tall.

MANY OCEANIC islands formed when molten rock from underwater volcanoes solidified into a platform above the waves. If the volcanic island is located far from the mainland, it is only by chance that plants and animals arrive on their shores. The first plants to arrive on an ocean island are either those with seeds so light that they can be carried far on the wind, or else those with seeds, such as the coconut, that can float in water. Very occasionally, land-birds may be carried in a storm far from the mainland and deposited on the island. Even more rarely, a breeding pair may be carried together in the same storm.

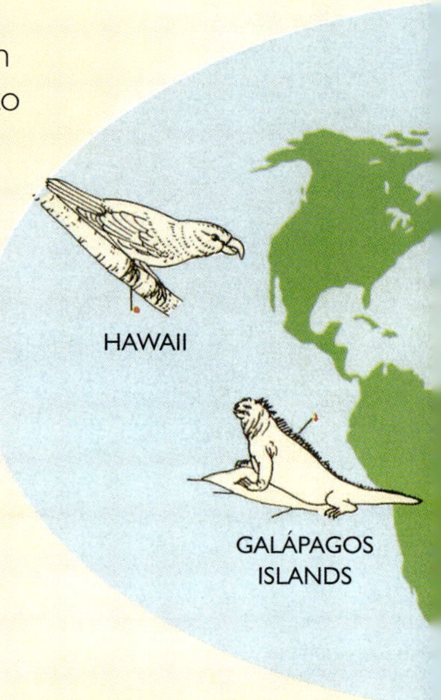

The Galápagos Islands
Some of the most famous examples of island life are those on the Galápagos Islands. In the three million years of their existence, the islands have gained a few stray reptiles – including tortoises that have developed into giant forms, snakes, and large iguana lizards that have taken to a life partly in the water.

THREE ST HELENA ISLAND TREES

The dodo of Mauritius was the size of a turkey, its body weighing more than 20 kg. Dodos became extinct in the 1800s as increasing numbers of people arrived on the island and killed them for food.

THE DODO OF MAURITIUS

Miniature animals
Sometimes big animals have had to evolve into smaller forms in order to cope with a limited island food supply.
This happened in the last million years on a number of islands. At times of lower sea levels, elephants and hippos walked to the islands from mainland Africa and Europe. They were stranded when sea levels rose again. In order to survive the loss of plant food, they evolved into small forms, no bigger than deer.

ELEPHAS FALCONERI STOOD LESS THAN 1 M HIGH

Adapting to island life
Once an insect or bird has arrived on an island, the wings that allowed it to fly there can become unnecessary if there are no natural enemies from which to escape. Flying insects adapt to become insects without wings. Birds become large and flightless, like the dodo of Mauritius or the moa of New Zealand *(see pages 36-37)*. Without larger enemies, small island animals can evolve into larger forms. A small lizard on the islands of Komodo and Flores in Indonesia grew into the Komodo dragon, a lizard as big as a crocodile.

MARINE IGUANA FROM THE GALÁPAGOS ISLANDS

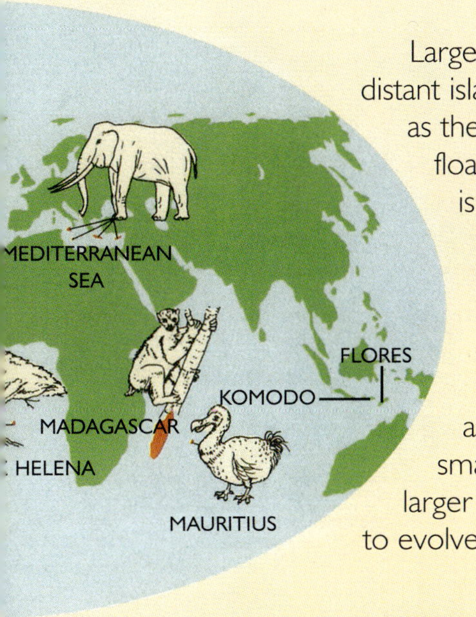

Large animals are the least likely to arrive on a distant island. Smaller animals are more likely to do so as they may be carried far across the sea on a floating tree trunk, for example. However, there is little chance of any animal making a successful journey. Those animals that do succeed have probably been very lucky rather than skilled in some way.

If there is enough plant food, the new arrivals will survive, and over many generations the small animals, without fear of larger predators, have the chance to evolve and become bigger.

Refuge on Madagascar
The island of Madagascar was once part of the African continent, but broke away more than 100 million years ago. For a long time, animals and plants moved to and from the mainland, perhaps through a range of islands in between. Between 20 and 30 million years ago this connection broke, stranding lemurs on the island. Lemurs in Africa died out with the arrival of monkeys. Monkeys did not reach Madagascar, where lemurs still live today.

MEGALADAPIS: THE LARGEST KNOWN LEMUR, NOW EXTINCT

HAWAIIAN FINCHES

The finches of Hawaii
The most remote of all the Pacific islands are those of the Hawaiian chain, formed by volcanoes that rise from the ocean floor. They are some of the most distant from the nearest continent: 3,200 km from North America and 5,500 km from Japan. Of all reptiles, amphibians and mammals, only one (before humans) has colonised the islands – a species of bat.

Until humans introduced them, there were not even any ants on Hawaii! In the whole history of Hawaii, less than 100 million years ago, a pair of breeding birds has arrived on only 15 occasions, providing all the birds now living on the island. One pair of finches from North America has evolved into a whole range of different types of bird, each with a beak specialised for a particular supply of fruit, seeds or insects.

Almost nothing in Earth's history has had such a dramatic impact on the pattern of life than the sudden increase in the population of just one of the animals: *Homo sapiens*. Instead of being subject to the environment, humans learnt to create artificial environments just to satisfy their needs. Through farming, humans cultivated those animals and plants that provided the best quantities of food, and removed all the competing types. An area of 2 sq km, with its original plants and animals, would have provided scarcely enough food for a single family of grazing humans. With modern intensive farming methods, the same land can now feed 2,000 people.

HUNTING

Hunting and herding
Early humans hunted for their food, moving from place to place in pursuit of the great herds of animals that roamed the African savannah grasslands. Gradually, people began to realise that it was possible to control the movement of the animals on which they relied for food. They would light fires to trap the animals, or build thorn fences with which to surround them. Once humans began to learn how to domesticate animals and plants, they no longer needed to live a nomadic existence, chasing after their food. Instead, they were able to build permanent settlements.

HERDING

The purpose of farming

THE aim of farming is to increase the available food supply. This, in turn, has allowed the human population to expand.

This map shows where certain animals or crops were first domesticated or cultivated. Domesticated animals and cultivated plants require protection because domestication has often removed their natural resistance to predators and pests. In the past century, farmers have fought a battle with the insects that come to eat or infect their

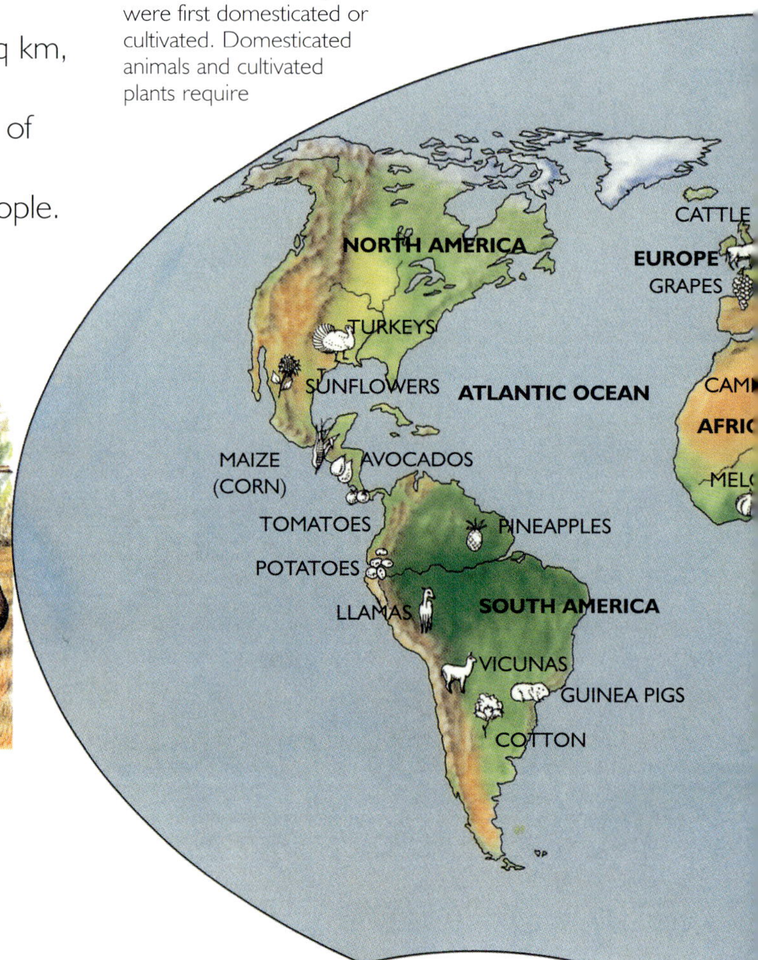

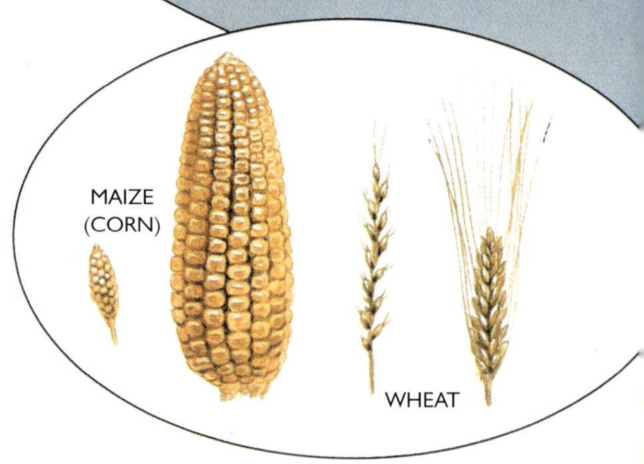

BEFORE AND AFTER CULTIVATION

Cultivating plants improved the size and quality of the fruit or grain. Evolution has created plants that are able to thrive in a particular environment.

Cultivating has simply concentrated on enlarging the seeds of plants like Indian corn and einkorn wheat, in order to make more food.

crops, the farmers using powerful chemicals that cause damage to other plants and birds beyond the farm. The destruction of forests and grasslands for agriculture replaces the natural plants and animals with those that people use for food. In this way much of the world's natural environment has been destroyed. Wherever there are rapidly expanding human populations more and more land is taken into agriculture, and the rich biodiversity of plants and animals is gradually lost.

Animals were soon employed as a source of power. This carving from Babylon is about 3,000 years old. It shows two oxen pulling a plough to create a furrow, into which a man is throwing seeds.

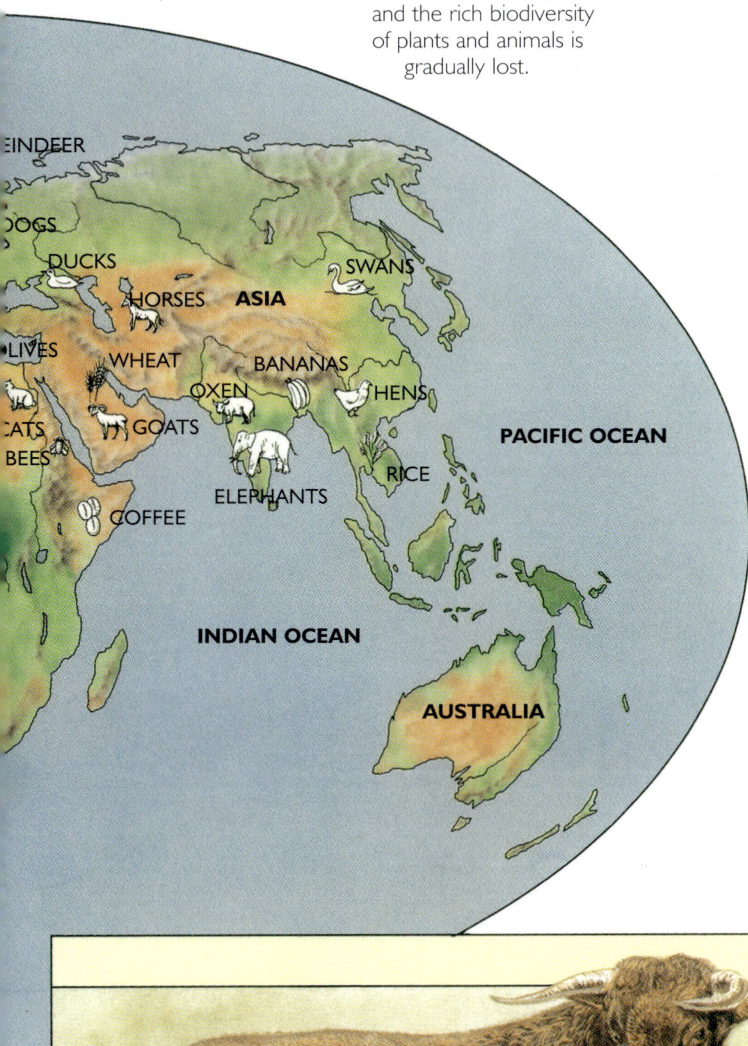

The common ancestor of dogs

One of the best examples of the power of breeding to create new shapes and sizes of animals is shown by dogs. All breeds, from the poodle to the Great Dane, are descended from wolves that were domesticated by our ancestors more than 10,000 years ago. The Alsatian and the husky have evolved least, and are little more than tamed wolves. When human beings use dogs to gather sheep or to hunt, they are relying on the dogs' natural instincts, carried from their wolf ancestors.

Domesticated animals

ANIMALS were carefully selected for domestication. Those animals which showed the desired properties: obedience and fearlessness for a hunting animal, a calm nature and good meat and fur for a food animal; obedience and strength for a pack animal, were bred to produce more animals. These animals were selected again and again until, after hundreds of years, herds of animals had been created that would live peaceably alongside people.

The first animal to be domesticated was the dog, to help in hunting and to guard the cave or hut. Then when grazing and farming began, first sheep and goats, then pigs and cattle were domesticated. Five thousand years ago, animals such as the donkey, horse and camel were domesticated in order to carry loads. Domestication is not at all easy: in the past 2,000 years, only the guinea pig, rat and hamster have been domesticated.

Human adaptability

Humans have been able to survive in many extreme environments on Earth. From the frozen Arctic to the highest Andes, humans have adapted to their surroundings. Ever since humans first watched birds in the air, and fish in the rivers, they have treated new environments as a challenge to be overcome.

HUMANS LIVE IN THE FROZEN ARCTIC

HUMANS LEARNED TO HUNT

FINDING WATER IN THE DESERT

MAKING CLOTHES

BUILDING SHELTER

The map of the future

IN 50 million years' time, the geography of the Earth will look very different. For example, the Atlantic Ocean will be almost as wide as the Pacific Ocean. There may also be lines of volcanoes along the fringes of the Atlantic Ocean, through western Europe and the coast of North America. Australia will have joined Asia to become one continent, and a great range of mountains will have replaced the islands of Indonesia. Asia itself will have a new sea cutting across Siberia, and another new sea will extend south from the Red Sea through East Africa.

The biggest unknown for the future of life on Earth is what will happen to humans.

Climates of the future

Twenty thousand years ago, the whole of Canada and northern Europe lay under thick ice. One day the ice caps will return. However, in the next few centuries climates are likely to become hotter as a result of the changes in the atmosphere caused by the 'greenhouse effect'. So, in the future, Canada could become a land of ice or desert.

Winners and losers

FIFTY million years ago life looked very different. What will life on Earth look like 50 million years into the future?

Some animals such as the crocodile, look much the same today as they did 200 million years ago. However, animals which are too dependent on a single food supply, like the bamboo-eating giant panda, are unlikely to survive any change in climate.

People have destroyed much of the world's natural forest and replaced it with two new environments: the field and the town. Some animals have benefited from this: rabbits, rats and mice live in the fields, pigeons nest on buildings and gulls scavenge on rubbish tips. Perhaps it will be the descendants of the animals that live alongside people that will create a wide range of animal types in the future.

Unlike animals and plants that have evolved over thousands of generations to cope with the conditions around them, humans have employed their intelligence to improve their natural abilities. Where there is extreme cold, instead of evolving thick, warm fur, people have stolen the fur coats of other animals, such as bears or sheep, in order to protect themselves. In the desert, people have dug deep wells to find the water that the cactus can reach only by growing deep roots. Unable to run as fast as most grassland animals, humans first developed skills of surprise and ambush, built traps, and used stones and wood to construct weapons. Later, humans rode on the backs of fast horses and finally built machines that could travel faster than any animal.

Future evolution

In the modern world, rodents are highly successful. In the future, they could evolve into giant forms, with rats becoming as large and fierce as wolves.

The most extraordinary acts of evolution will continue to occur on ocean islands. Giant flightless birds and bats may emerge, and more land animals may take to the water.

ANIMALS OF THE FUTURE? GIANT RABBITS, MICE AND RATS

One day, humans may even leave their home planet, Earth, and set up colonies in space. However, physically and mentally they remain the same people who emerged out of hundreds of thousands of years of evolution, when life was short and hard and there were many natural enemies. Humans remain connected to a time when they lived in trees and a time when they evolved a universal in-born fear of, for example, spiders and snakes.

EVOLUTION OF EARTH LIFE
MILLION YEARS AGO
1,500
1,400
1,300
1,200
1,100
1,000
900
800
700
600
500
400
300
200
100
TODAY
ALGAE
FLOWERING PLANTS
CONIFERS
GINGKOS
FERNS
CLUB MOSSES
HORSETAILS
ALGAE
INSECTS
CRUSTACEA
SPIDERS
MOLLUSCS

Descended from a common ancestor, all the different types of plants and animals are connected branches on a tree of life.

GLOSSARY

Adaptation Some feature of an animal or plant that helps it to survive in a particular environment, such as the hard shell of a tortoise for protection or the long neck of a giraffe for feeding on high branches.

Algae Tiny plants, each made up of only one cell.

Amphibian A group of animals, including frogs and newts, that spend most of their life on the land but lay their eggs in water.

Ancestor A past relative of an animal or plant, linked through its parents and its parents' parents, sometimes through thousands or even millions of generations.

Asteroid A lump of rock measuring up to many kilometres across, which travels around the Sun. Very occasionally, asteroids collide with the Earth.

Backbone The set of bones, or vertebrae, that joins the arms and legs of an animal to its head, and which provides the support necessary for movement.

Bacteria A group of primitive single-celled organisms that can live without oxygen. They survive in some extreme environments, including the boiling springs on a volcano.

Carnivore A meat-eating animal.

Cartilage A material that looks and feels like plastic. The bones of a shark are made of cartilage. It is also found in smaller amounts giving support to the skeletons of other animals.

Cell The smallest unit of most living organisms.

Climate The combination of temperature and rainfall averaged out over many years. Climate governs the range of animals and plants that can live in any region.

Cold-blooded Animals, such as reptiles and fish, that cannot keep their blood at a fixed temperature. Instead, their blood temperature heats up or cools down according to their surroundings.

Coniferous Trees that produce their tiny seeds inside wooden cones. Most of them do not lose their leaves in winter.

Continent The largest land areas, such as Asia, Australia and America. They are made up of thick masses of rock that rise higher than the surrounding ocean floor.

Continental shelf The area of shallow sea, generally less than 1,000 m deep, found around most of the continents.

Coral Tiny sea animals, known as polyps, that live together in enormous colonies and create a rocky skeleton on which to grow.

Deciduous Trees that lose their leaves, in the autumn of each year, and grow them again in spring.

Descendant A relative of an animal or plant, linked through its children and its grandchildren, sometimes through millions of generations.

Environment All of the surroundings of an animal or plant, including the climate, land and water, and other animals and plants.

Equator An imaginary circle around the Earth, halfway between the North and South Poles.

Evolution The gradual change of living things over many generations. Animals and plants adapt to their environment. Evolution is most rapid when the environment itself is changing.

Extinct	A species of animal or plant no longer alive today.
Fossil	The remains of an animal or plant preserved in the soil or rock.
Genetic code	The chemical instructions that exist in the living cell, which instruct an animal or plant how to grow and how to live.
Glacial period	A time of colder climate, when thick ice sheets covered northern Europe and Canada. The last glacial period ended about 10,000 years ago.
Herbivore	An animal that eats plants.
Herd	A group of large animals, usually herbivores, that live and feed together.
Ice Age	The name given to the last two million years, when about every hundred thousand years there has been a glacial period lasting several tens of thousands of years.
Inhabitant	An animal or plant that lives in a particular location or environment.
Invertebrate	An animal without a rigid backbone, such as a worm, spider or crab.
Land-bridge	A narrow land connection between the continents, such as Panama which joins North and South America.
Life-form	Any living creature, animal or plant.
Living fossil	An animal or plant alive today that is almost the same as one alive millions of years ago.
Marsupial	A group of mammals, in which babies are born so small and helpless that they are looked after inside a pouch on their mother's abdomen. Marsupials include kangaroos and koalas.
Nectar	A sweet liquid produced by flowers to encourage insects, such as bees and flies, to visit and so to carry pollen to another flower.
Organism	Any living animal or plant.
Palaeontology	The science of fossils and of past life.
Population	A group of animals or plants that live in the same region.
Predator	An animal that hunts and eats other animals for food.
Prehistoric	Something that existed thousands, or even millions, of years ago.
Prey	An animal or plant that is hunted or eaten by another.
Placental mammal	An animal that gives birth to well-developed live young, and that suckles them with milk from the mother's breast.
Pollinate	To carry pollen from one flower to another. This allows seeds to develop which will eventually grow into new plants.
Primate	The group of mammals that includes monkeys, lemurs and people.
Primitive	Something that has a very old and simple form.
Reptile	A group of cold-blooded, vertebrate animals that lay eggs, usually on land. It includes crocodiles, lizards and snakes.
Savannah	Regions of low rainfall and bushy vegetation, found in the interiors of the hotter continents, such as Africa and South America.
Sea level	The height of the surface of the sea. Over many thousands of years the sea level changes, in particular as a result of water becoming trapped in ice sheets during glacial periods.
Supercontinent	As the continents move slowly across the Earth, they have once or twice combined to form a supercontinent. The last supercontinent, known as Pangaea, existed around 200 million years ago.

INDEX

R

S

T

U

V

W

Z